Prosecuting Jesus

Prosecuting Jesus

Finding Christ by Putting Him on Trial

Mark Osler

WJK WESTMINSTER
JOHN KNOX PRESS
LOUISVILLE • KENTUCKY

First edition
Published by Westminster John Knox Press
Louisville, Kentucky

16 17 18 19 20 21 22 23 24 25—10 9 8 7 6 5 4 3 2 1

Book design by Sharon Adams
Cover design by Eric Walljasper

Library of Congress Cataloging-in-Publication Data

Names: Osler, Mark William, author.
Title: Prosecuting Jesus : finding Christ by putting him on trial / Mark
 Osler.
Description: First edition. | Louisville, KY : Westminster John Knox Press,
 2016.
Identifiers: LCCN 2015047264 | ISBN 9780664261856 (alk. paper)
Subjects: LCSH: Osler, Mark William. | Christian biography--United States. |
 Christian biography--United States. | Jesus Christ--Trial--Drama.
Classification: LCC BR1725.O738 A3 2016 | DDC 277.3/083092 [B] --dc23 LC record
available at https://lccn.loc.gov/2015047264

Most Westminster John Knox Press books are available at special quantity discounts when
purchased in bulk by corporations, organizations, and special-interest groups. For more
information, please e-mail SpecialSales@wjkbooks.com.

In memory of Benjamin and Marie Lewis

Contents

The Trial of Jesus, 2011–2014

4/14/2011	Minneapolis, Minnesota	University of St. Thomas
4/16/2011	Richmond, Virginia	Church of the Holy Comforter
1/15/2012	Chicago, Illinois	4th Presbyterian Church
2/7/2012	Cambridge, Massachusetts	Episcopal Divinity School
2/27/2012	Jefferson City, Tennessee	Carson-Newman College
3/18/2012	Nashville, Tennessee	St. Henry's Catholic Church
3/25/2012	Oklahoma City, Oklahoma	Westminster Presbyterian Church
8/22/2012	Minneapolis, Minnesota	University of St. Thomas
10/9/2012	Virginia Beach, Virginia	Regent University
10/17/2012	Pasadena, California	Fuller Theological Seminary
10/18/2012	Azusa, California	Azusa Pacific University
3/26/2013	Boulder, Colorado	St. John's Episcopal Church
3/28/2013	Austin, Texas	First Baptist Church, Austin
11/8/2013	New Orleans, Louisiana	Loyola University
11/10/2013	Baton Rouge, Louisiana	St. George's Catholic Church
2/23/2014	Tucson, Arizona	Grace/St. Paul Episcopal Church
4/13/2014	Manchaca, Texas	Manchaca United Methodist Church

4885 Harvard Road, Detroit

(photo courtesy of Mark Osler; used by permission)

Introduction

*F*or some of us, it matters where you are from. I'm from Detroit, and now I'm a part of the diaspora of uprooted people, black and white, from that city. In Minneapolis, where I live now, I will meet someone new and find they are from Detroit, and we will start talking about our high schools and looking for connections. It has happened with the guy at the auto shop and with my congressman, Keith Ellison.

There is a wistful tone to those conversations. Often, we both feel compelled to explain that we left because of a job or to go off to school or because of a relationship. There is a warm fog around it all, an inability to see it clearly, because we don't want to. For many, the neighborhoods they came from are literally gone, the houses torn down and carted off and the fields full of tall, brown grass. Carrying around this vague, almost indefinable sense of loss makes it easier to do something like advocate against the rolling tragedy of a flawed death penalty—it gives us something to attach our grief to as we move forward. Once we do that, once we find a cause or a faith or an art we can hold and see, we can be remarkably whole and strong. Detroit is a visual city, not a literary one, and so are its people. "It's only true," one Detroiter told me, "when I see it."

When I was born, my family lived on Harvard Road on the east side. Our block was full of sturdy little homes full of families and kids, many of them Belgian. Our own house was a tidy two-story with big windows that looked out on the sidewalk. The neighborhood was bounded by East Warren Avenue, a busy street lined with small stores and offices. I loved to play in the tiny backyard with my brother, Will, or ride my rickety blue tricycle down the block to where my friend Jeff Plansker lived; at dusk I noticed that the moon seemed to be following me home, encouraging me. When you are four, the whole world is right around you.

In 1967, though, the larger world took mine over. That is when the riots came, and much of the city burned—a rebellion swelling up from years of racism and disappointment in a city and nation divided by race. It began when the police broke up a party for two black veterans returning from the Vietnam War. Over 1,200 people were hurt or killed, and over 2,000 buildings were destroyed. President Lyndon Johnson sent in regular Army troops to restore control after the Michigan National Guard and local authorities had failed. Like hundreds of thousands of other people, my family moved to the suburbs in the wake of that destruction.

I grew up just outside that city as it then fell apart, year by year, block by block, as we watched from a safe distance like spectators at a demolition derby behind the metal screen. I kept going back, though, pulled to the chaos and uncertainty by an unseen force. I have always been drawn to stories imbued with deep meaning.

First, after college, I worked as a process server and errand boy in the city itself, out of a small law firm on the fringe of downtown. Later, after law school at Yale, I came back again and lived with my brother in an apartment perched on top of a parking garage overlooking old warehouses and factories. At night I could hear sirens from the streets and birds in the grassy fields that had reclaimed the land that industry had abandoned. There was a richness to those sounds, a music to it, that I can still hear.

During the day, I wore a suit in a Detroit courtroom high in the federal courthouse. On trial or being sentenced, typically, was a young black man, often still a teenager. Seated at counsel table one afternoon, the defendant was trying to look tough, but the fear showed through. I was working; it was my job as prosecutor to put him, like thousands of others like him, in prison for selling crack.

The prosecutor gets the table closest to the jury, and we were taught to leverage this advantage by stacking up evidence at the front of the table. In this case, that evidence was simple: a cheap gun disabled by a plastic loop through its barrel and a handful of plastic bags holding small, white rocks. Those were my tools; they were what I had to define this young man as a "crack dealer." That's what prosecutors do, after all; they define a person, at trial and at sentencing, by the worst things that they have said and done. In the nineties, a crack dealer was possibly the worst thing a person could be, with the possible exception of a "crack whore."

On that afternoon, once the defense was done putting on what little evidence it had, it was time for me to make my closing argument. I buttoned the jacket on my blue suit, nodded to the court, and faced the jury. In this kind of case, I usually said about the same thing, regardless of which black man sat in judgment. "You know, five grams of crack may not seem like much," I would say, holding the plastic bags in the palm of my hand, "but one hit of crack can weigh as little as one-tenth of a gram. That means that what I have in my hand here could be fifty hits of crack—fifty rocks that will be smoked by someone's daughter, someone's son, someone's mother." At this point I would turn and look at the defendant. "That's what he was doing; selling crack. He's a crack dealer."

The jury would then look at the defendant like they were looking at a murderer. I knew that I would win, and I usually (though not always) did. I wasn't a very good prosecutor, but it didn't take a really good prosecutor to win that kind of case. When the jury would come back and the foreman would pronounce the defendant "guilty," I felt no leap of joy within. It was just a tragedy on top of a tragedy, and I knew that, at least in that spare moment.

Eventually, I had enough of tragedy. I went from trying cases to teaching students how to do it. It wasn't easy to get a job as a law professor after practicing law for ten years (in the legal academy, practical experience is often a liability when job seeking), but Baylor Law School in Texas was willing to take a chance on me. I started teaching there in 2000 and showed future prosecutors how to stack up the evidence at the front of their tables, properly authenticate a business record, and cross-examine a hostile witness.

Baylor is a Baptist school—the largest in the world—and working there forced me to define my own faith. I mean that quite literally: as part of the regular interview process, I met with the president and provost of the university for an extended discussion of my beliefs. I passed that test, but perhaps only by hiding my own uncertainties. I was not as sure of Jesus' requirements as they were; I didn't see the directive rule giver that they did, but I didn't have a firm vision to replace it.

Apparently, it wasn't too hard to notice the wobbly nature of my faith. Midway through the events described in this book, a gifted writer named Abby Rapoport followed me through much of the substance of my life. She visited my classes; talked to my students, my priest, and my family; and came to a church (First Covenant in Minneapolis) where I was giving a sermon. In the profile she later wrote for *American Prospect* magazine, she observed,

> Covenant isn't his church, and he doesn't fully fit in here. He also doesn't quite fit in at St. Stephen's Episcopal church, where he currently worships, nor did he quite fit in at the Baptist church he attended when he taught law at Baylor University and lived in Waco, Texas. It's unlikely he was a perfect match for the Congregational church he was raised in or the Quaker meetings he sometimes joined when he was in his twenties.[1]

I first read that passage while lying on the worn green couch in my office, and it hit me hard. I sat up and read it again. She had dug out a secret and made it plain. How could she know my inner discomfort in church when I thought that fact was hidden? After all, I have always intentionally made church a part of my life. In elementary school, a teacher suggested to my parents that they should take me to church, since I talked about God a lot, and they did. Since then I have been a part of many congregations, have played many roles in those churches, and even took up the leadership of the Association of Religiously Affiliated Law Schools. Not fitting in with my church didn't jibe with the way people thought about me, or so I imagined.

Abby was on to me, though. In every church I had been a part of, there was some discomfort, a painful gap between what was taught or assumed and the hard truths I read in the Gospels. My heart and my eyes told me that the Jesus of the Gospels was deeply troubling, a disrupter more than a comforter to people like me. Rarely did my churches talk about that troublesome Jesus who calls on us to cut

---

1. Abby Rapoport, "The Quality of Mercy," *The American Prospect*, March/April 2014, http://prospect.org/article/quality-mercy-0.

against the patterns and habits of our world—the man who told the wealthy ruler to give away everything he owned to the poor. When I felt most dislocated was walking out of church feeling vaguely contented and ready for lunch. It didn't fit. When Jesus left those he had taught, they often were afraid or confused or troubled or ecstatic with joy. His was not a way of quiet comfort.

The truth was that I had never found a Jesus that seemed real in any of those churches; they had not been able to describe an idea of God on earth that didn't seem contrived or backward or twisted in knots. I understood the lessons they taught, and I believed that Jesus lived, but I couldn't *see* it. I needed that kind of definition: a Jesus so real that I could see him.

This book is the story of how I got there. In the end, to find a Jesus I could see, I had to prosecute him—that is the way I knew to define people. That's what I did, in eleven states over the course of three years, before audiences that were large and small, conservative and liberal. It began in a well-appointed courtroom in downtown Minneapolis and ended in Manchaca, Texas.

In the beginning, though, I imagined that it was simply a project about the death penalty. I am a long-time opponent of capital punishment and wanted to push for the abolition of that sentence in the United States. It's not a reflexive or sympathetic position for me—I am a former federal prosecutor who believes in the incapacitation of dangerous criminals—but a belief rooted in my faith.

I was frustrated, though, with the few encounters I had with the anti-death-penalty establishment. Primarily, they seemed to talk to one another at conferences and rallies, and that wasn't very good advocacy. After all, you can change someone's mind only if he or she doesn't agree with you in the first place. I wanted to take a message about capital punishment to the places where people actually believed in executions—and in the United States those places include Christian schools and churches in states like Texas and Virginia.

There is something deeply ironic about the enthusiasm many Christians have for the death penalty. The central narrative of Christianity, after all, is about an unjust execution, and Christians proudly wear the execution device—the cross—as a symbol of their faith. At the very least, one would expect those who worship a man who was executed to take the problem of executing others very seriously. The connection between the crucifixion and capital punishment became clear to me one Sunday morning not long after I started teaching at Baylor.

That morning, I woke up and opened the *Waco Tribune-Herald* to find the report of an execution in Huntsville, not too far away. The prisoner was a murderer, someone who had killed a child or a police officer or an innocent store clerk. Before describing the crime, though, the article first detailed the last meal the condemned man had requested before his execution. It was probably something typical: a cheeseburger, a Dr. Pepper, a cupcake. The whole thing, the terrible crime, the little meal on a tray, the tragedy of all the deaths, struck me as unbearably sad. There was no victory in any of it.

Then I went to church. I was a member of Seventh and James Baptist Church, a moderate and engaged congregation on the fringe of the Baylor campus. It was, as usual, a place of reprieve, the kind of place where so many people knew the words and music that only about half needed a hymnal when we sang. It was Communion Sunday, something we celebrated only once a month. The Communion plate was passed down to me, and I took the bit of bread and held it in my palm. It felt heavy in my hand. I looked down, and in that spare, short moment I saw it: this thing in my hand represented the last meal of a man who knew he was about to be executed. It was the liturgical equivalent of that cheeseburger, Dr. Pepper, and cupcake.

That juxtaposition was yet another awkward thing to carry with me out of church, like a stone in my shoe while I walked. I knew that this odd combination or social belief and religious narrative meant something, but I did not like the clear meaning: that Christ had something in common with the murderer. That just didn't seem right. One was impossibly bad; the other, impossibly good. How could there be an intersection between the two? There is a simple answer to that paradox and a more complex, challenging one. The simple answer is that what the perfect and the utterly flawed share is food and the table around which we gather, all of us. We all must eat. The complex answer is what this book is about and largely what the last decade of my life has been dedicated to. Like most hard questions, the best answer lies within a story rather than an argument. And that story took me to a truer self, one that sees the strength and truth and light in Jesus the disrupter.

The project that epiphany eventually led to was this: In under two hours, we would conduct the sentencing phase of the trial of Jesus under the procedure and rules of the state we were in (subject to a few necessary adjustments). It wasn't really a play, because there was no script. It is probably fairer to call it a trial, because that is what we know, and that is how we treated it. We presented witnesses drawn from the Gospels and performed all the other aspects of the trial, from opening statements through closing argument. At the end, we divided the audiences, large and small, into groups of twelve to deliberate as juries and return a verdict. This was the trial we would take from Pasadena to Boston, and Minneapolis to Austin.

I didn't do it alone, of course. Former and current students pitched in, and I faced the same opponent every time: Jeanne Bishop, a veteran Chicago public defender and global advocate against the death penalty. In retrospect, what we shared was a thrill ride through many of the diverse varieties of American Christianity. It probably was not an accident that my primary collaborators—Joy Tull, Sara Sommervold, David Best, and Jeanne Bishop—were all natives of the frontier West rather than the coasts, with a certain fierceness to each of them.

The experience was intense, complex, and often very dark. And, in the end, there was this: we would watch the people of that church or school as they left the building, greeting them and thanking them for coming. Some would comment on the proceeding or shake my hand, but all of them looked troubled. Really, there is no other word for it than "troubled." Only rarely did someone say we changed his or her mind or assert that we didn't. Instead, they all seemed lost in thought. There is a good in that. In the realm of my passion, troubling the waters is the best I can hope for, a first step toward change and a sharing of my own soul's hue.

It all came from someplace, of course. The last time I went by that little house on Harvard Road, I had to stop my car and catch my breath. My son John was with me, and he looked over at me anxiously, knowing something was wrong. Following my eyes, he saw what I did: the rough plywood boards covering the windows. It might be, I thought, that the owners were just doing a renovation, or maybe there was an accident that blew out those windows. But that was not what my heart suspected. We sat for a moment in quiet and then went on, away from that place and toward the rest of the world.

Chapter 1

Minneapolis

I'm a teacher, and often what I teach is advocacy. Part of what I teach my students is a truth that I learned slowly and through my own mistakes: people usually change their minds because of stories, not arguments. No one has ever pulled up in traffic at a light, read a bumper sticker, and decided that he or she had been wrong about an important issue. Instead, we change our minds over time, and usually that process starts with a story about ourselves or someone else that challenges a core belief or idea. We don't change our minds when someone argues at Thanksgiving dinner about same-sex marriage; we change when someone at that table tells a personal story about the person whom he or she loves.

This story begins with a college psychologist in Virginia named Craig Anderson. He has the rugged good looks of a man who has spent as much time as possible in the outdoors, his tanned face framing warm eyes and an easy smile. I met Craig when he hired me as a student worker during my junior year at the College of William and Mary. I wasn't really that good at my job, and Craig sometimes got angry calls from the dean of students. Still, we had a good rapport, and I realized right away that he was a natural mentor for me.

Craig dearly loves his church, Holy Comforter Episcopal. It is nestled in a woodsy neighborhood on Monument Avenue in Richmond. Monument Avenue, of course, is the famous Richmond boulevard that features enormous statues of confederate heroes: Robert E. Lee, J. E. B. Stuart, Stonewall Jackson, and Jefferson Davis are displayed astride horses, confidently looking into the distance. Holy Comforter, though, is beyond the area of these statues, literally and figuratively. It is, like many others, a church that is struggling to be modern, relevant, and traditional all at once.

Craig had told me about the church, and in the autumn of 2010 he began to ask if I wanted to present something there. I asked him what kind of thing, and his response was a somewhat frustrated "*Something*—you know, the stuff you do."

The "stuff I do" was in a little flux at that moment. It was my first fall teaching at a ten-year-old law school, the University of St. Thomas in Minneapolis, after a decade teaching at Baylor University in Waco, Texas. In the preceding year, I had published a book, won a case in the U.S. Supreme Court, and even found myself turned into a character in a movie (*American Violet*). The Supreme Court case (*Spears v. United States*) had been the culmination of years of work fighting against a pernicious sentencing rule that directed the same term of incarceration for one gram of crack and one hundred grams of powder cocaine. The court's opinion held that judges could "categorically" reject that ratio embedded in the federal sentencing guidelines. The next year (2010), Congress changed the law and the guidelines. That project was deeply satisfying but also left a void once it was completed—I was the dog that had caught the car and couldn't quite figure out what to do next.

Craig's idea was a good one. I knew what he hoped for: a unique, compelling challenge to conventional thinking that would draw people into his church. The easy answers—a sermon, a lecture I had given before, an advocacy workshop—were not sufficient. Craig wanted and deserved something brand-new. Pondering his challenge, I realized with a jolt and a little dread what the right thing was for Holy Comforter. I needed to revive the trial of Jesus.

I had done the trial once before, in 2001. At that time, I was a new professor at Baylor and a mere drop in the intellectual ocean that was my home church, Seventh and James Baptist. Seventh and James was known as the most intellectual church in a town full of theologians, and that reputation was well earned. My small adult Sunday school group there, for example, contained an English professor, an archeologist, a graduate student in education, an Old Testament scholar, two seminarians, a costume designer, a linguist, and . . . me. It was led by Professor Bob Darden, who has almost single-handedly preserved the legacy of black gospel music. It was a pretty intimidating place.

In the summer, Seventh and James eschewed the regular Sunday school program in favor of something called Chautauqua, based on the famous intellectual camp in upstate New York. Chautauqua was a fascinating series of short classes on a variety of topics, reflecting the remarkable range of expertise among the membership of the church. In one recent summer, for example, classes were offered in Religion and the Civil War, Spiritual Lessons from People Who Kill, Aramaic Christianity, and Art and Faith in the Writings of Michael Mayne. It takes a lot to show the good people of Seventh and James something they don't already know.

My idea for a Chautauqua presentation was inspired by the morning described in the introduction, the morning that I realized that the Eucharist was the celebration of the last meal of a condemned man. "Why not," I thought, "jam faith and politics together and try Jesus here in our church?"

And so we did. My first job was to find a partner in the project, someone to play the opposing counsel. Since I would be creating something adversarial, I needed precisely the right adversary: someone who knew the Gospels, who knew the rules of evidence, and who was an able practitioner in the courtroom. My background and natural inclination are on the side of the prosecution, so I sought out a defense attorney.

The perfect candidate was working in the office next to my own. Bill Underwood is a tall, imposing man with a heart for social justice. At Baylor Law, he was in charge of the Practice Court program, a mandatory part of the third-year course of studies. "Brutal" is a fair description of Practice Court, which requires students to devote nearly all their waking hours to the classes and exercises designed to make them into well-honed trial lawyers. As head of the program, Bill taught the students for several hours each day and then grilled them as they performed courtroom simulations in the evening. He excelled at this difficult task until 2005, when he became the interim president of Baylor. In 2001, Bill Underwood was the best lawyer in Waco, and he agreed to be my opposing counsel.

For four weeks we engaged that congregation in an epic legal battle—choosing a jury, presenting witnesses, and arguing the merits of our cases. Debating the death penalty there amid that congregation was not a purely academic exercise; among the faces looking back at us were two male church members who had served as the forepersons of separate juries in real death-penalty cases tried in Waco. Both had led juries that had voted to impose death.

The searing heat outside was matched by the intensity of our trial, and the philosophers, deans, opera singers, and assorted academics in our audience launched into the discussion with a passion. In the end, this messy, lengthy success was both exhausting and satisfying. There were problems, of course. We had included every phase of the trial, including jury selection, which bloated the time frame without adding value. More problematic was our choice to present the first part of a capital trial—the decision on guilt or innocence—which got bogged down in the question of exactly what constituted blasphemy in the modern day.

It was the intensity of that trial in Waco that I remembered as I searched for an answer to Craig. If what he wanted was for his church to grapple with faith's response to a contemporary social-justice issue, putting Jesus on trial for his life in Richmond seemed the perfect fit. Virginia has put more people to death in its history than any other state; the first execution in the future United States took place there, in 1608. In recent years, Virginia has ranked third in the number of executions carried out. The idea of doing it again, and far from home, was daunting. For a week, I told myself that it was too much—that I needed to focus on making things work at my new job above all else. I did not have the time or energy to become Christ's prosecutor again. But the idea kept coming back to me, unbidden. I didn't want it to be, but I knew that it was the right path. I called Craig and hoped he wouldn't answer.

Which, of course, means that he did. I launched into a broad description of the Waco trial and what we might do with that idea in Richmond. I wanted to shorten it and limit it to consideration of sentencing and let the entire audience deliberate rather than just a chosen jury. As I spoke, I could imagine him nodding and smiling at the other end. With some friends, you know how they feel even when they are silent. When I was done, he asked the single most important question: "Who will be the defense attorney?"

I told him that I would get back to him on that. Bill Underwood had become the president of Mercer University in Georgia and was unlikely to be able to take the time for the project. I was in a new place and did not know any of the lawyers in Minnesota well enough to ask such a huge favor.

The trial would not work as a one-man show. I was about to appeal to Craig to canvass the congregation when a sharp memory came to me. In November of 2010, not long before Craig asked me to come up with an idea, I had attended an anti-death-penalty gathering in Atlanta. I was giving two lectures at the conference and was wrapped up in my own preparation. Even so, I had met some fellow travelers among the hundreds of advocates from all over the country.

One of them was Jeanne Bishop, a public defender in Chicago. I had first seen her in Atlanta as she walked arm in arm with Sister Helen Prejean. Jeanne was a willowy, elegant figure with dark hair and was leaning in intently to hear what Sister Helen had to say. She was there with a group of murder victims' family members, people who had counterintuitively come to oppose the death penalty for the very people who had created such great personal loss. They were the ones who could answer the challenge "You wouldn't feel that way if it were your brother or sister or mother or father," as indeed it had been their brother and sister and father and mother who had been killed for no good reason.

Later, Jeanne introduced herself as we sat in the pews at Ebenezer Baptist, Martin Luther King Jr.'s church on Jackson Street in Atlanta. I asked her for the story behind her advocacy, and she told me about it in the gentle soprano voice of the church singer she is every Sunday at Fourth Presbyterian Church in Chicago.

The story began in a busy, happy house with a mother and father and three girls. Of the three sisters, Nancy was the happy, sunny one, the girl who loved shopping and cooking, singing around the piano, decorating for the holidays, and telling groan-inducing jokes. The baby of the family, she was adored, the one who could get away with anything once she flashed her trademark grin, eyes sparkling. One of the people Nancy loved most was a dark-haired young man she met at work: Richard Langert. Richard grew up in a Southwest suburb of Chicago, the youngest of four boys in a strong Catholic family. He was strong, too, a varsity athlete at his high school who stood at six feet three and weighed 230 pounds. His teammates nicknamed him the "Gentle Giant."

The two of them meshed perfectly. Richard was solid and soft spoken where Nancy was bubbly and chatty. She sat with him in the stands of Comiskey Park to watch his beloved Chicago White Sox play baseball; he sat proudly in the front row when she performed in a downtown play. They got the book on life early. They married in their twenties, when Nancy was only twenty-three, and started out right away trying to have children. When Nancy got pregnant at the age of twenty-five, they were ecstatic.

Most of the family—Jeanne, her parents, and Nancy and Richard—met up in downtown Chicago to celebrate. The dinner took place on the night before Palm Sunday, April 7, 1990, at a snug Italian restaurant on Clark Street. It was the kind of place made for a happy gathering—a big table laden with steaming bowls of pasta and bottles of wine and lots of laughter and light. As they hugged good-bye outside, Jeanne told Nancy, "See you tomorrow." As Jeanne later explained in her book *Change of Heart*,[1] it is a sentence she no longer uses, because you never know if it will be true.

Nancy and Richard returned to their home in one of the most affluent and safest towns in Illinois, the North Shore suburb of Winnetka. At the same moment, a sixteen-year-old named David Biro was using a glass cutter to break into their home and rechecking the loaded gun he had stolen. Though they both were from well-off Winnetka families, David Biro was the opposite of Nancy in many ways. She was full of light, and he was dark and violent. He had tried, and failed, to kill others before. One attempt involved lighting another child on fire. He had tried to poison his own family by tainting their milk; he was sent briefly to a psychiatric institution after that incident.

When Nancy and Richard walked through the front door of their townhouse, Biro was waiting. He pointed a .357 magnum revolver at them and led them to the basement. Once there, he put the gun to the back of Richard's head, execution style, and fired. Nancy, horrified, saw her husband collapse on the floor. Biro turned on her and fired twice, striking her in her side and abdomen, bullets tearing into her pregnant belly. Then he ran out, leaving Nancy to die along with the child she carried.

The coroner who performed the autopsy on Nancy's body surmised that she had lived for a short while after being shot. Marks on

---

1. Jeanne Bishop, *Change of Heart: Justice, Mercy, and Making Peace with My Sister's Killer* (Louisville, KY: Westminster John Knox Press, 2015).

her body and the trail of blood she left on the basement floor show what she did in the brief time she had left on earth. First she pulled herself slowly backward, using her elbows, to a metal shelf and then banged on it with an ax, again and again, trying to call for help. No help came. In her dying moments, she dragged herself to where her husband's body lay. She dipped her finger in her own blood and wrote a message: the shape of a heart and the letter "u," her short-hand for "I love you." She died there beside him and her last words, a last message of love. Biro took nothing; he came only to kill.

In the wake of the killing, Jeanne's own life was turned upside down. Before Biro was found to be the killer, the FBI had launched an investigation of Jeanne's political activism, thinking that some-one from Northern Ireland had somehow killed the wrong sister. Biro was given three life sentences, without the possibility of parole.

Some people, of course, thought Biro deserved the death penalty, but Jeanne Bishop was not one of them (at any rate, Illinois law did not allow the death penalty for juvenile offenders). Over time, she became active in a group called Murder Victims' Family Members for Human Rights, which gathered together people like Jeanne to argue against the death penalty. As part of that group, she had spoken across the United States as well as in Japan and France. At the same time, she maintained a full schedule as a public defender in Cook County, Illinois, representing Chicago's indigents accused of a vari-ety of crimes, and she sang in her church choir.

Jeanne Bishop seemed to be the perfect choice for defense attorney—given her vocation, her advocacy, and her faith—leaving open only the question of whether she would have the time and inter-est in such an unusual project. When I called to ask her if she wanted to do it, though, she had only one question: "When will we start?" Her voice was tense with excitement. At some deep level, she under-stood the project I hoped to create.

When I called Craig to tell him that I had found a defense attor-ney, he was cautious but intrigued. I sent him a few articles about Jeanne's work, and that spurred him to do more research on his own. He uncovered the wealth of difficult experience hidden in Jeanne's life: her choice to leave a lucrative law practice to become a pub-lic defender, her hardships after the death of her sister, and even the unauthorized play that was written about her and performed in

Chicago over her objections. With a few more calls, we were booked to perform the trial in Richmond in April.

Looking toward this new reality, I feared the unknown. We were going to be trying a new kind of presentation in a far-off place before people we didn't know, using witnesses we had never met. It seemed too much all at once. We needed a practice run before we plunged into the capital of the Confederacy and its pro-death-penalty culture.

My own school, St. Thomas, seemed like it could be a safe haven for a low-key practice run. My first semester had gone well, a welcome change from the pressure cooker of Baylor, and I was ready to show off a little. I approached my dean with the idea, and he readily agreed. St. Thomas takes seriously its mission, which is described in a single sentence: "The University of St. Thomas School of Law, as a Catholic law school, is dedicated to integrating faith and reason in the search for truth through a focus on morality and social justice." Because Catholic social teaching runs against the death penalty in the United States (where there are secure prisons that can ensure incapacitation), the trial was a natural fit for the school.

I didn't pretend, though, that doing the trial in Minnesota was a good piece of advocacy. Good advocacy happens only when you have a chance of changing something, and Minnesota rejected the death penalty over a hundred years ago. The idea of capital punishment offends the Scandinavian sensibilities of the place. When I describe in my sentencing class the death-penalty process in Texas, my Minnesota students have a remote fascination, as if it were a purely sociological exercise. "Why do they think it is a good idea?" is a frequent question, as if we were studying a tribe in Borneo rather than the people directly south of us on I-35. This trial would be for practice, to make sure that it worked.

To prepare for the trial, Jeanne Bishop made a visit to St. Thomas a few weeks before the April 14, 2011, event date. I was going to be busy with class and other duties during much of her visit, so I tasked one of my students, Sara Sommervold, to be her liaison.

Sara stood out in the first-year Criminal Law class for a number of reasons. She was a nontraditional student, having taken a dozen years off of school to pursue acting, to work at a variety of fascinating odd jobs worthy of David Sedaris, and to start a family. Her life experience gave her a certain confidence that is rare in law students, and she also possessed a sense of justice that was remarkably unfiltered. In class one day, as I described a particularly troubling bit of legal doctrine, she threw both hands straight into the air over her head and exclaimed, "That's just wrong!" It was not only a physical gesture I had previously seen performed only by Kermit the Frog; it also reflected a deep revulsion at injustice.

Sara was a daughter of South Dakota who had attended a high Episcopal church in Sioux Falls. Her mother had been a creator of the arts scene there, bringing theater and other performances to a downtown area that now features the Mary Sommervold Hall that was named for her. Sara, like Jeanne, grew up in a home imbued with musical theater and (like Jeanne) is prone to burst into song at unexpected moments. Who better, then, to shepherd Jeanne Bishop around? Sara picked Jeanne up at the airport and careened back to school (neither woman likes to actually steer the car while driving because it negates the ability to gesture wildly with both hands), and Jeanne almost immediately invited Sara to become her trial partner.

Now that Jeanne had someone to work with, I felt compelled to find a partner of my own. Among litigators, such trial partners are often referred to as "second chairs" because they sit in the second chair away from the client at counsel table. They not only perform some of the tasks of the trial itself—typically the opening statement and some of the examinations of witnesses—but also offer an important second set of eyes to take in all that is happening in a trial.

For that role, I chose Jonathan Scheib, a student in my Criminal Practice class for third-year students. Jon was a sharp student, a natural in the courtroom, and devoted to pursuing a career in criminal law. He agreed immediately, and now the lineups were set. Sara also lined up several students to play the roles of witnesses, seeking out those who had both a bit of acting ability and some level of biblical understanding. Because much of the trial is extemporaneous, one of the keys to success is having witnesses who know well the stories we will ask about. This is especially important on cross-examination, when one of us might ask about aspects of the event that no one had previously considered. It was all, by plan, unscripted.

Our judge was to be Hank Shea, the Harvard-trained ex-prosecutor who was a faculty colleague at St. Thomas. To call Hank an "ex-prosecutor" is like calling Michael Jordan a "former basketball player." When I was with the Department of Justice and thereafter, Hank was a legend for having brought a series of white-collar criminals to justice. More than anything, his presence on the faculty assured me that St. Thomas was a place where criminal law was taken seriously. From the beginning, Hank was a supporter of the project and brought needed gravity to our first run.

Jeanne and I from the start treated this trial the way we would any other, meaning that we gave no advantage to the other side. We did not compare notes; we did not reveal our theories; and Jeanne did not even say whether she would have the defendant, Jesus, testify on his own behalf. This quietness was natural to us; the practice of criminal law is largely extemporaneous, unlike civil litigation where the entire enterprise is based on months of depositions and other discovery. Criminal lawyers often have to fly blind. We are not actors; we are trial lawyers.

Because we were preparing for the trial in Virginia, we used the law and procedure of that state. As in Texas, the key question for the Virginia sentencing jury is whether the defendant poses a risk of "future dangerousness." If the jury feels he or she does and that mitigating factors don't outweigh the reasons supporting execution, then a death sentence will issue. My job then, as prosecutor, was to describe Jesus as *dangerous*. All of our evidence, and that of the defense, had to be drawn from the Bible.

The task of describing Jesus as dangerous, once I focused on it, was surprisingly easy. He told rich people to give away all their money; he promised to divide families; and he insulted the religious authorities of his community. He even went on a rampage in the Temple itself. I just needed to bring evidence for his dangerous activities through eyewitnesses.

Just before the trial was to begin, I was sitting at the desk in my office at the law school, a few floors up from the moot court room, making last-minute notes about how I would introduce the event. Jeanne sat across the room on a couch, quietly absorbed in her own notes. Suddenly Hank Shea popped his head in the door with news: "The members of the board of governors are here today for a meeting," he said, referring to the body that oversees the law school. "They moved their meeting around to see your trial." He smiled and headed off.

Jeanne shot me a stricken look. Usually fairly calm and confident, her voice tightened as she said, "Board of governors? I was worried enough about disgracing you in front of your students and faculty colleagues; now I have to worry about disgracing you in front of the big donors, too! You just started teaching here a short while ago— aren't you even a little worried about taking this risk?"

The truth is, I was. Because it was a practice round, I did not expect a big crowd in the ceremonial courtroom off the atrium. I was wrong. When we arrived for the trial, every seat was taken. Lining one wall, dressed like the successful lawyers and judges they are, were the members of the school's board of governors. Joining them were most of the student body and many of the professors, including Catholic lay leader Susan Stabile, pro-life activist Teresa Collett, and law-and-religion expert Tom Berg. The atmosphere was electric.

One constant of criminal trial work is the uncertainty of what will end up being important. Because so much cannot be planned—for example, what the other side's witnesses might say—there is a fluid dynamic that requires attentive listening and the ability to adjust. Only as a trial develops does anyone, including the lawyers and judge, know what facts or people will matter most to the jury and in what way. This trial was no different.

Sara had recruited a first-year student, Phil Steger, to play the role of the prosecution's central witness, the apostle Peter. Peter's importance to the trial lay in the fact that he was a witness to everything in Jesus' ministry—he was almost always present. This need was made more prominent, I found later, by Jeanne's choice not to call Jesus to testify. At first, I thought that it was an odd decision. Jeanne, however, was being consistent with her practice as a public defender, and over time it came to make sense. I realized after a few rounds that if given the chance, I could undo a church member forced to play the role of Jesus on cross-examination.

I had heard great things about Phil, an older student who had theological training and a fascinating career as a peace activist prior to coming to law school. He wasn't unusual at St. Thomas in that way, but he stood out even there for his intelligence and conscience. My heart sank, though, when I saw Phil headed to the courtroom. He was wearing jeans and a hoodie—apparently he had forgotten that he was supposed to testify in court. I cut him off midway across the atrium.

"Phil! You're testifying in a half hour!" I looked down at his hoodie disapprovingly.

Phil shrugged. "I'm playing Peter, right?"

I nodded.

"Well, he's a fisherman." I looked at him blankly. He gestured at his clothes. "This is what I wear to go fishing." In my rush to get everything pulled together, I didn't have time to straighten him out. As the attorney calling him as a witness, it was my responsibility to make sure he was dressed for court, preferably in a suit and a tie. Watching him walk away toward the courtroom, I bit my lip as I pondered how poorly I had done that part of my job.

As it turned out, his instincts were much better than mine. When it came time to call my first witness, it was with some trepidation that I called out the name "Simon Peter!" In response to my call, Phil leaped to his feet and eagerly trotted to the front of the courtroom. There was a huge, puppy-like smile on his face. When he took the oath, he leaned forward, listening intently to the words. Every bit of him seemed impatient to tell the story of Jesus.

His body language did not lie. As the prosecutor, my job was to make Jesus appear dangerous, and to accomplish this I had studied the Gospels to find the passages that seemed darkest. Among these, I relied heavily on Jesus' promises to divide families and his insistence that material possessions could impede faith; after all, we would rather think that our faith will strengthen our families and make us rich. In my lengthy examination of Phil-as-Peter, I went to the well of Scripture time and again and confronted him with Jesus' own words. Each time, he eagerly verified what I had quoted, with a look of astonishment and love and an admiring glance at the defendant. At one point, I pulled out one of the most difficult passages to hear: "So, Peter, you were there weren't you, when the defendant said, 'I have come to set a man against his father, and a daughter against her mother'?" (see Matt. 10:34–35).

Phil nodded eagerly. "The master said that!" He gazed again at the defendant and shook his head slowly. "So often, we did not realize the wisdom of his words at the time he was saying them." Again and again this was repeated, as the apostle fervently and enthusiastically agreed with every confusing thing Jesus said. It was a transformative moment for those of us in the room. *Of course* that was what Peter was like! He was the eager follower, a genuine worshiper, whose enthusiasm made him seem clumsy at moments like the transfiguration. There, Peter sees Jesus' true nature, standing beside Moses and Elijah, and responds by offering to build them huts. Huts! Phil had captured the essence of that character in a way that no sermon could describe. With his performance, I first realized the true power of this form of presentation. We could make this old story new.

Some might complain that Peter didn't really testify at Jesus' trial, and it is a fair complaint. However, it does seem that Caiaphas, the prosecutor, would have wanted to call him. After all, we know that Caiaphas's servant girl went to Peter and asked if he knew Jesus. Given the context—Peter was sitting outside of the trial, and Caiaphas was frustrated with the witnesses he had—it could be that the servant's mission was to round up further witnesses. Peter escaped the role of witness against Jesus by denying (three times) that he knew him at all. Had he not denied knowing Jesus and appeared at the trial, he may well have been like Phil Steger—the living spirit of what we had just seen. I didn't really know what Jesus looked like (probably not like the students we used for this exercise), but I had a much better idea of what his follower, Peter, would look like. Phil had brought me closer to what I sought by what I could see reflected in his eyes as he testified.

When Phil stepped down from the stand and walked back to his seat, there was a hush. I turned to look back at the crowded room, and one word came to me: *church*. This was what church should be like—people challenged and surprised by what they had heard and then left silent. It had happened in a school, my school, because of what a student had done.

There was a reception planned for the board of governors at the time the trial concluded, so I headed up there with the others who were involved. One after another, they approached me and took my hand in both of theirs and told me how impressed they were with the students, with Jon and Phil and Sara. I nodded and smiled and realized that it was the best thing they could possibly leave with: the idea that our students could do great things.

It is fitting that the first religious community we went to on our tour of American Christianity was the one I call home. Doing the trial steps from my office let me see the deep and powerful issues of faith my school engages in from within the Catholic tradition. I knew, with certainty, that I was in the right place for this project.

With this first time, the template was set. We knew that the trial would bring surprises. We knew that we would learn more than we taught. We knew that there was an eager, engaged, fascinating audience of faith ready to see it. And, finally, we knew that it was going to take us to some interesting places. As we walked out of the building, one of the students ran up to me. "You're doing this other places, right? Because you *have* to!"

I nodded and looked east. We would do it again, in Richmond, in just two days.

Church of the Holy Comforter, Richmond, Virginia
(photo courtesy of Mark Osler; used by permission)

Chapter 2

Richmond, Virginia

*R*eturning to Virginia was not a simple thing for me. As an eighteen-year-old three decades before, I had arrived to attend college at William and Mary as a complete outsider who knew nothing about the South. That first night, the guys from my dorm walked together to the cafeteria a few hundred yards away. Soon after we had left the dorm, I realized I was far in front of everyone else. I waited for them, and it happened again; I simply had to get used to a different pace than the one we had in Detroit, where things moved fast and life had a certain edge. Over time, I learned to walk more slowly, listen more carefully, and speak more gently.

When we performed the trial in Virginia, fascinating classmates and teachers returned to my life. One of them was Tom Brooke, the laid-back senior who ran the campus radio station and gave me a show after I impressed him with a remixed version of Minnie Riperton's song "Loving You" (I added dogs, cats, lions, and elephants to the tweeting birds in the background of the song, with fighter jets dive-bombing the menagerie at the end).

Another formative figure from Virginia (who, like Tom, was destined to reappear in the course of my work on the trial) was Professor Joanne Braxton, the poet who had taught my African American literature class at William and Mary. She challenged me in any manner of ways; when there was a slave-owner part to read, she made sure I was the reader. She returned my essays and asked for more depth, and she often responded to my points in class with a precise and difficult question, offered with a half-turned head and only the hint of a bemused smile. The rumor was that she lived in a house by a stream in the "necks" of land outside of town, in the wild parts of the county. I believed it; I could see her there in a place slightly wild, even though I knew that she was preparing to defend her doctoral dissertation at Yale. She made me want to be a teacher.

In contrast with Professor Braxton's cool demeanor was the unmistakable laugh of government professor Ron Rapoport, whom you could hear through several walls. He was tall and gangly, brilliant and enthusiastic, and talked like no one I had ever heard. His lectures were furious strings of truth. In time, I learned that his accent was from his childhood home in Waco, Texas.

Then there was Craig Anderson, my boss in my work-study job in the dorms. He was, like me, a hockey player. He was from Boston, went to Colgate for college, and then moved to Virginia for his later work, but he always kept a Boston heart. He drove a Ford Ranger pickup truck, a vehicle he needed to haul his bike or kayak on one of his many outdoor excursions. Like professors Braxton and Rapoport, Craig challenged my thinking every time I saw him. Each suggestion was clothed in gentleness, though—even when I deserved something more caustic. Over Christmas break, for example, I made the mistake of storing my poorly maintained motorcycle in a closet below my apartment, where it predictably leaked oil. The dean of students, outraged once again at my antics (we had a history of this), contacted Craig in a lather about my poor decision.

When I returned to campus, I could tell something was wrong when I saw Craig. I had gotten him in trouble with his boss; another person might have fired me on the spot. His comment, however, was classic: "Maybe you should have thought that one through a little more." Maybe!

This was the Craig Anderson, looking much the same nearly thirty years later, who brought the trial to his church in Richmond. He wasn't satisfied with just one presentation, though; he wanted us to come to Richmond prior to the trial to talk about the issue and explain our backgrounds. We agreed, and plans were made for a pair of appearances on March 5 and 6. On Saturday night, we would address the public and the church about our project, and then on Sunday morning I would give a sermon from the pulpit while Jeanne sang with the choir.

As I had come to expect with Craig's ideas, there were some significant challenges embedded in this plan. I'm not a trained minister and had only spoken from a pulpit once before. More significantly, Jeanne and I were awkwardly paired to speak on the same bill. I'm a prosecutor by nature, and she is a defense attorney; we see things through different eyes. She also was a thoroughgoing Chicago progressive while my years in Texas had made me more of a political moderate. Most important, perhaps, was that we differed in some of our core beliefs about criminal justice—beliefs that no doubt had sent us on different trajectories professionally.

One of these differences involved the sentence her sister's killer had received, though there we cut against type as I took what would be perceived as the more liberal view. Among my academic interests was the peculiarly American sentence of life without parole for defendants who committed their crimes as juveniles (often referred to as Juvenile Life without Parole, or JLWOP). My opposition to that sentence flowed from a biblical passage my mother had taught me at a young age—Micah 6:8, which instructs, "He has shown you, O mortal, what is good. And what does the LORD require of you? To act justly and to love mercy and to walk humbly with your God" (NIV). As a prosecutor, I found it impossible to reconcile the values of justice and mercy if justice is to treat similar people alike (i.e., for sentencing purposes) and mercy is about giving someone unearned grace. To do one negates the other. The best answer that I had was that law should not be all justice or all mercy—that at the very least there needed to be some aspect of both available. I opposed JLWOP for the same reason I opposed the death penalty: because there was no room for mercy in those sentences.

I had been pulled in sideways to the debate on that issue. In 2009, I received a letter from the chair of the House Judiciary Committee, asking me to come to Washington, DC, and testify at hearings on a bill to get rid of JLWOP. I eagerly accepted the offer, and as I prepared my argument, I began digging up materials—speeches, rallies, newspaper editorials—some of which had been written by Jeanne Bishop.

It was a memorable morning. Congressional hearings are, in real life, much as they are portrayed in movies (at least on high-profile or controversial issues). The members of Congress sit in tiered seats at the front of the room, with aides at the ready behind them. Visitors and media sit behind those who testify, and sometimes (as was the case that morning) more of the crowd stands at the back. The witnesses sit before microphones, facing the interrogators. I brought along two of my students to help and observe; they looked on intently.

Though Democrats controlled the House at that time and had convened the session, for some reason only a few attended, while the full complement of Republicans was there and eager to begin. Their aides buzzed around them; one came over to say hello, as she was a former student of mine. Once the session began, though, it was all business. I became committed to my position on this new issue.

Jeanne, on the other hand, had a perfectly good reason to take the opposite view and support JLWOP. That was, after all, the sentence that David Biro had received after killing Nancy Bishop; her husband, Richard; and their unborn child. She did not want it disturbed. While I had known the weight of judgment as a prosecutor, I did not know the pain of such loss.

One of the things that Jeanne had committed to was never to say publicly the name of Nancy's killer. To do so, she thought, would mean that the killer would be remembered, and she understandably wanted it to be a story about and in memory of her beloved sister, her brother-in-law, and their unborn child. In fact, shortly after meeting Jeanne for the first time, I had to look up the killer's name because she had never mentioned it. Shortly before our trip to Richmond, though, something began to shift.

Jeanne had told me that she was working on a book about forgiveness. In fact, she was doing research on that book in Atlanta when I met her. Her coauthor was John Boyle, a remarkable minister at her church who as a young soldier in WWII had helped liberate the Nazi death camp at Dachau. I'm no expert on forgiveness, but I know someone who is: Randall O'Brien, the president of Carson-Newman University in Tennessee. It occurred to me that I needed to connect these two people.

I had met Randall when he was the chair of the religion department at Baylor. It was my first semester there—in fact, my first month living in Texas, my first month as a teacher in any capacity, and my first month in such a thoroughly Christian environment. I had an idea: I wanted to teach a class that used the techniques of Baptist preachers to help law students construct more compelling arguments. They were, after all, similar enterprises in that both the preacher and the trial lawyer are using discrete facts and morality based on a text to lead people to specific decisions.

People had told me that Randall O'Brien was the best preacher in town, so I decided to ask him to co-teach the class with me. In retrospect, it was a bold move—a newbie professor going to the head of Baylor's strongest department with a request to co-teach a class. At first, Randall seemed a little surprised, but he quickly said yes. For several years, the two of us (along with Truett Seminary preaching professor Hulitt Gloer) taught hundreds of Baylor students how to construct a convincing argument that Texas juries would respond to. It was in those class sessions that I learned how to give a sermon (something I now do several times a year); Gloer and O'Brien were masterful.

Randall later became the provost of Baylor and then took the job heading up Carson-Newman. We stayed in touch, and I made a point of reading his work periodically, including his book *Set Free by Forgiveness*.[1] I also had pored over a very short article about forgiveness he had written for a Baylor publication, *Christian Reflection*.[2] It was this article that I sent to Jeanne to consider for her own work.

Not long after she got the article, Jeanne called me, angry (or at least as close to angry as Jeanne Bishop gets). "Have you read this?" she asked.

I replied that I had.

"Do you know what he says I should do?" She did not wait for me to answer. "He says that when you forgive, you need to then have a relationship with that person, reach out to them. It's backwards! He should be reaching out to me!"

It was true. Randall's (and Christ's) radical notion of forgiveness did require a personal reconciliation. When the prodigal son returns home, after all, having squandered his inheritance and having sullied the family name, the father is the one who runs into the field to greet and welcome him back. Still, this is not what the upset Chicago lawyer on the other end of the phone wanted to hear.

---

1. Randall O'Brien, *Set Free by Forgiveness: The Way to Peace and Healing* (Grand Rapids: BakerBooks, 2005).

2. J. Randall O'Brien, "Forgiveness: Taking the Word to Heart," in *Christian Reflection: A Series in Faith and Ethics* (Waco, TX: Baylor University, 2001).

"Listen," I suggested, knowing that the task was better suited to someone more qualified, "why don't you call Randall?"

"I can just call him up?" She seemed incredulous. "A college president? What will he say?"

In fact, I knew exactly what he would say. He would first go on for a while about how she was doing wonderful things and how he understands how she must hurt, and he'd say that she probably knows her own situation better than anyone else does and that she doesn't need any advice other than her own. Then, after that, he would challenge her to do things she absolutely did not want to do. And that, apparently, is exactly what happened when Jeanne called Randall O'Brien, the author whose words had so affronted her. They talked for hours.

When we got to Richmond and met with Craig Anderson and his wife, Lori, at their house prior to the presentation, Jeanne was quieter than before. I assumed that, like me, she was nervous about the new type of presentation we were going to give. We had agreed that we would trade off—I would begin by speaking about the death penalty generally from a prosecutor's perspective; then she would take over and discuss the interests of a victim's family member; and then we would both talk about the project yet to come, the trial of Jesus in that same sanctuary.

After dinner, we walked into the church for the first time. It is an archetypical Episcopal church, with hard wooden pews, kneelers, a vaulted ceiling, and choir benches and an elevated pulpit in the front. No one had arrived yet, so we blocked out where we would stand and sit. Since both of us are trial lawyers, we usually do not need a microphone except in very large spaces; at any rate we both tend to wander around a lot as we speak.

Slowly, the people of the church filtered in. They were old and young, rich and poor, black and white, gay and straight—a diverse crowd relative to what is found in many American churches. Some sat tentatively in the back, while others came right up to the front. By our starting time, we had a decent crowd who, like us, did not know what to expect.

Going first, I introduced myself and spoke briefly about my own evolution of belief on the death penalty. It's not complex; much of my opinion is framed by the bare fact that Jesus came upon a legal execution (of the adulteress in John 8:1–11) and told the people there that they did not have the moral authority to kill her (" 'Let anyone among you who is without sin be the first to throw a stone at her,' " v. 7). Along with poverty, it is one of the few contemporary social issues that Jesus confronted directly. Moreover, when he advised that we visit those in prison (see Matt. 25:36–40), he didn't say the innocent in prison or the political prisoner but rather those honestly condemned. How can we do that if we kill them?

When I was done, I nodded to Jeanne, and she stood and strode to the front. She is tall and cut a striking figure as she stood straight before the crowd and gathered her thoughts. The room fell quiet, and then she began as I expected, by telling the story of Nancy's life and death. People became utterly still when she got to the hardest part of that story, where she describes the killer lowering his gun to shoot Nancy in her pregnant belly, leaving her to die next to her husband. There is this moment, right then, when Jeanne looks to the side, trying not to cry. This time, she succeeded.

It was then that something different and remarkable happened. Jeanne looked up at the stock-still crowd. "I need to do something tonight I have never done before," she said in a voice raw with emotion. There was a still, small moment before she continued: "At the beginning of every church service at my Presbyterian church in Chicago, before we do anything else, we publicly confess our sin before God and one another. We pray a prayer of confession. And my confession is this: I have gone twenty years without speaking the name of the person who killed my sister and her husband and their baby. I wanted his name to die and Nancy's and Richard's to live. That was wrong. He is a child of God. God loves him." And then she said his name. Without faltering, she said, "His name is David Biro."

It is striking what a simple act can do. When we say a name, we acknowledge the humanity of another person, and they are known. Somehow, with those few sentences, Jeanne was able to pack in all the meaning of that act—in a way, she spoke David Biro back into being. People left the sanctuary that night emotionally exhausted. Later, Craig turned to me and asked, "Did you know she was going to do that?" I shook my head, and we laughed as we walked into the humid, fragrant night.

This set the table for our presentation of the trial the next month. We flew straight to Richmond after the practice run at St. Thomas, landing in the gentle and familiar warmth of a Virginia spring: the smell of flowers and a shedding of jackets that wouldn't hit my northern home for weeks.

We returned to Holy Comforter as familiar figures and were greeted warmly. Our first order of business was to meet and prepare our witnesses. Craig and other leaders of the church had recruited parishioners to play the witnesses in the cases. The recruits looked anxious as they waited for us to finish blocking out the staging for the trial—figuring out where the witnesses would sit and where we would present our arguments. Glancing over, I tried to figure out who would have each role. There was one participant I could not quite figure out.

He was a young black man, probably around sixteen or seventeen years old. He fidgeted on his seat, shifting uncomfortably on the hard bench as he waited to be interviewed, his mother stolid beside him. The other participants chattered away, but he kept to himself, obviously uncomfortable.

Jeanne saw him, too, but unlike me she figured it out right away. This young man was to be our Jesus. She told me later what her thought process was at the moment that she had that realization: that this Jesus looked and acted like her clients back in the dank lockups of Chicago. His mother, there with him on the wooden plank, was Mary. It transformed the trial. Something about it, seemingly, turned the switch on her passionate public-defender persona, the part of her that fought hard for people like him.

Jeanne's energy only made my job harder. I prepared my own witnesses with the same goal I had in Minnesota—to make Jesus seem like a threat to the wealth, traditions, and families we hold dear. Peter was always the hardest witness, in large part because I could not prepare him for his testimony the way I could others. Because he was a hostile witness (after all, he was pretty committed to the defendant's side), I did not have the right or (sometimes) the ability to talk to him until he actually took the stand, and the most preparation I ever got was just a general outline of the events I might discuss. That made it a particular challenge; it is always harder flying blind.

The evening of the trial, the sanctuary was not jammed full, but I was pleased with the crowd. Most intriguingly, many of those in attendance were not members of the congregation and were probably not opponents of the death penalty. They were precisely the kind of people I wanted to reach. They spread out around the large sanctuary, seemingly wary.

One of the people in attendance was Eric Marrapodi, the editor of CNN's *Belief Blog*. He squirreled Jeanne away in the choir robing room for an interview prior to the trial, curious about how it would all work. His extensive piece for CNN would be the first written about the trial, and he did a remarkable job of capturing the shape and hue of it all.[3] It created a stir, too. Marrapodi's article went viral on social media and led to a favorable piece in a very unlikely place—Perez Hilton's celebrity gossip blog. Hilton described the event and closed by saying, "So based on current Virginia laws, Jesus would live! Hooray! Only to rot away in prison. Boo! At least he'd be alive to appeal. Ha! What do U think about this mock trial? Does it make U think twice about capital punishment?" At least he did not draw anything on the picture of Jesus that ran with his article.[4]

Such conclusions were yet to come, though, as we reviewed our notes and waited for the judge to arrive. The judge has an important role in setting the tone of any trial, and this was never more true than in Richmond. The judge was William G. Broaddus, a prominent lawyer in Richmond and the former Attorney General for the Commonwealth of Virginia. He arrived only a few moments before the trial was to begin, just like a real judge, and brought with him his own surprise. He strode to the front of the room, positioned himself behind the podium, and cleared his throat with authority. A tall, lanky figure with swooping Brezhnev eyebrows, he has a bearing to him that brings people to attention. The crowd hushed and looked up expectantly. In a strong Virginia accent he directed them firmly, "Ladies and gentlemen, please stand up to be sworn in as jurors." Obediently, the crowd stood and raised their right hands. "Do you and each of you solemnly swear that you will well and truly try and a true deliverance make, and a true verdict render according to the evidence, so help you God?"

3. Eric Marrapodi, "Jesus on Trial: What Would a Modern Jury Do?" *CNN Belief Blog*, April 22, 2011, http://religion.blogs.cnn.com/2011/04/22/jesus-on-trial-would-he-be -sentenced-to-death-today/.

4. "Jesus on (Mock) Trial in Virginia," Perez Hilton (blog), April 23, 2011, http://perezhilton .com/2011-04-23-virginia-church-holds-mock-jesus-trial#.Vs4Wp5wrKVM.

I glanced over at Jeanne, who was as baffled by this development as I was. We had planned to finish this version of the trial by dividing the audience into groups of twelve for deliberation, but neither of us had ever considered the possibility of swearing in the jury. Broaddus, who knew his way around a courtroom, remembered this bit of procedure that we had forgotten. It mattered, too. As we learned with later experiences, the ceremony of swearing in the jury committed our audience to the experience and made their role crystal clear. Old Bill Broaddus knew what he was doing.

As I gave my opening, I felt something that had first emerged to a lesser degree in Minneapolis, a certain darkness of spirit. How could I not? It was the evening before Palm Sunday, the beginning of Holy Week, and I was making the case against Jesus. My role set the prosecutor within me against the follower of Christ, and that clouded my soul. It was a nearly indescribable feeling—in fact, deeply sad and slightly desperate. As I talked about how Jesus' own followers would testify that he would set mother against daughter, I felt that darkness settle in deep inside of me. It was a dangerous thing.

The anger at Jesus that came out in my voice was not artificial. It came from a lifetime where easy answers had eluded me; every time I thought I understood this man, I had been proven wrong. It was the kind of anger we feel against our parents but suppress—the unrighteous anger of a child that finally finds something to attach itself to. The excuse of prosecuting Jesus had become that something.

When I called Peter to the stand, I was full of resolve. By the time I gave my closing argument, the dark fury was fully engaged. I implored the jury to kill the defendant, lest he destroy our society. At the end, like Caiaphas the biblical prosecutor, I ripped my shirt in frustration, under the conceit that Christ would rip a similar hole in the fabric of society. That bit of theatricality, the tearing of the shirt, was a living out of a part of the story that made particular sense to me. Mark 14:53–65 describes the scene: After a number of witnesses conflict in their testimony, Caiaphas asks Jesus if he is the Messiah, and Jesus says, " 'I am' " (v. 62). At that point, "the high priest tore his clothes and said, "Why do we still need witnesses?" (v. 63), and Jesus is condemned.

While to a layperson the tearing of clothes may seem nonsensical, it reflected something that was in me as a prosecutor. After all, we put prosecutors in a unique and difficult role within society—it is their job to look someone in the eye and say that their freedom should be taken away, that they should be impoverished through fines and restitution, and, sometimes, even that they should die. There is a great emotional commitment in that task, one that flows from the job itself. After all, what if you are wrong in asking that someone's freedom or life be taken? It is a great responsibility to bear.

And still, the prosecutor must bear that responsibility and act with certainty. When that certainty is undermined by witnesses who conflict and who do not tell a consistent story, it creates an almost indescribable frustration. It is this wellspring of frustration that makes the tearing of clothes seem fitting, an outward manifestation of what is going on inside. It did not seem out of place to punch my fingernail through the oxford-cloth fabric of my shirt as I finished my argument: "If we let him live, he will tear a hole in those things that hold us together—our families, our economy, our safety—and all that we love will be torn." In that moment, too, I meant it.

It was, in the end, a little over the top, particularly in contrast to Jeanne Bishop's gentle and passionate argument in favor of the defendant, resting on the fundamental decency of his character. After we were done arguing and Judge Broaddus had instructed the jury, I was barely listening; my shrouded mood and emotional exhaustion had overtaken me. It was my first taste of the real and deep cost of this project. Outside the church, there was a small garden, and I walked out into the familiar scent of Virginia in the spring to gather my thoughts.

When I returned home to Minneapolis, it took several days before the unsettled mood within me began to dissipate. Jeanne's own return to Illinois was very different. A reporter from the *Chicago Tribune* called and asked for an interview and photo shoot. It was raining, so Jeanne took an umbrella with a penguin-head handle, and that's how they took the picture that appeared on the front page of the *Tribune* on Easter Sunday, above an article titled "Radical Forgiveness." The story it told was raw and true: that Jeanne had started a remarkable journey that would soon take her places she had never been.

There was, for her, a quieter and more meaningful moment as well. She went to a shop near her home in Winnetka, a leafy north-shore suburb of Chicago. Waiting for her there, having been placed in a dark-wood frame, was a precious piece of history. Jeanne had worked for years to end the death penalty in her home state of Illinois, and the preceding month she and her collaborators had finally succeeded. On March 9, 2011, Governor Quinn had signed a bill abolishing capital punishment after decades of debate, moratoriums, restarts, and exonerations. Jeanne was invited to the signing ceremony and stood by the governor as he explained his reasons, his hand resting on a Bible and a copy of Sister Helen Prejean's book.

After the ceremony, Jeanne was headed out of the statehouse, reflecting on the long road leading to this moment: the countless speeches in church basements, the circuitous trips to towns in the southern part of the state, the efforts to raise money for the cause, the many hopes that had been dashed, and the disappointments now transcended. As she started down the steps, she heard someone call her name, and she turned around. Coming toward her was an aide to the governor, breathless, with something in her hand. It was the dark brown pen, engraved with the governor's seal, that Quinn had used to sign away the lingering existence of capital punishment in Illinois. "He wanted you to have this," the aide said.

And so, somewhere in Jeanne's house in Winnetka, that pen rests in a wooden frame, a testament to what is possible.

Phil Steger as Peter at Fourth Presbyterian Church in Chicago
(photo courtesy of Fourth Presbyterian Church; used by permission)

Chapter 3

Chicago

*F*or nearly eight months after Richmond, other projects consumed me. I had been busy on a number of fronts. Perhaps most important, I had started the nation's first law school clinic dealing with federal commutations, a use of the constitutional pardon power that allows the president of the United States to shorten the sentence of a prisoner while leaving the conviction in place. My motivations for pursuing this work were the same as what pushed me toward the trial of Jesus. The pardon power is the only clear inclusion of a deeply Christian principle—mercy—in the structure of the Constitution. Building a new program from the ground up was difficult work. It had begun heel to toe with the end of a prior multiyear project: convincing the Supreme Court that sentencing judges should be allowed to reject the harsh sentencing guidelines for crack cocaine, guidelines that provided the same punishment for one gram of crack or a hundred grams of powder cocaine. The day after President Obama's first inauguration, January 21, 2009, I won the case of *Spears v. United States*. Clarifying an earlier ruling in *Kimbrough v. United States*, the Supreme Court held that judges could "categorically" reject that guideline.

The *Spears* case, despite being a split decision that overturned circuit law, was decided without argument, so the decision came as a surprise—but the best kind of surprise. It was the talented former student who worked with me on the case, Dustin Benham, who told me about the decision, and I was elated. There was some irony in it, of course—the guideline I had challenged was one that I had relied on myself as a prosecutor. It served as the basis for sentences

I sought, very long sentences, against low-level offenders who were always (at least in my cases) African American. I had been a part of the problem and had been able to become a part of the solution.

For a moment, and it was only a moment, I laid down on the green couch in my office, closed my eyes, and let myself appreciate it. Then the phone rang again. It was a trailblazing law professor from Ohio State, Doug Berman, who had worked with me on the project that led up to *Spears*. Berman, a Harvard-educated sentencing expert, presciently set up the first blog in the field before a series of major cases changed everything in the mid-2000s. The first thing I did when I turned on my computer in the morning was to check in with Doug's blog, *Sentencing Law and Policy*.

Berman is also a fast talker and not much for formalities. Slapped out of my reverie by the ringing phone, I answered it only to hear Berman's shocking first sentence: "So, what are we going to do next?" The answer was clemency, and particularly the president's potential ability to use commutations to shorten the sentences of people serving time under the shaky 100-to-1 ratio. Presidents in recent times had failed to use the pardon power in that way, even when sentencing rules were changed. President George W. Bush had granted only eleven in his two terms, and one of those was for former White House aid Lewis ("Scooter") Libby, a far cry from the hundreds granted by many of his predecessors.

Taking on Berman's challenge, clemency was a project I was approached at both the retail level (through the clinic, where we helped individual clients) and at wholesale. In league with a key collaborator, legendary reform advocate Nkechi Taifa at the Open Society Foundation, I was able to meet four times with members of the president's Domestic Policy Council to press for clemency reform. The White House visits combined with a writing campaign, and I was able to place pieces with CNN, MSNBC, and a number of newspapers. I was doing my best to put the issue before the right people, but it also pulled me away from a focus on the trial.

Nor was that all that was adding tumult to my life. A new area of social justice demanded my attention. As with crack and overincarceration, a problem I had helped create as a prosecutor, it was an issue on which I had been on the wrong side. For much of my life, I was a casual bigot—not even aware of the toxicity of my own words.

Like most boys of my age, I grew up throwing around the pejorative word "fag" in the general direction of those who seemed different. I laughed with the other guys about, and sometimes at, boys who seemed to be gay. It was bullying, and it was wrong.

For much of my young life, those ideas went unchallenged by my friends and my church. Only in college did I come across a strong countervailing voice. That voice belonged to George Greenia, a Spanish professor at William and Mary. He, virtually alone, stood up for and supported gay students in what was then a virulently anti-gay environment. He spoke up gently, firmly, and consistently and was vilified for it in some quarters of town. I did not know him, but when I saw what he was doing it gave me pause.

In law school, I came across others who spoke up like George Greenia, albeit in a more conducive environment. At Yale Law, I was even befriended by a handful of gay men and lesbians, who were able to overlook some of my stupider questions and comments. Their friendship changed my views. I stopped thinking about being gay as some kind of defect and accepted it as simply a difference. That shift, though, did not extend to thinking critically about what prejudice meant. I took a job at Baylor, for example, knowing that the school expressly discriminated against gay men and lesbians, who were barred from employment there and threatened with punishment as students by the student code of conduct. The discrimination against people like my law school friends was open and obvious, but I took the job anyway. It was, sadly, not something I saw as "my issue."

Nor did I worry about it much as I spent ten years teaching at Baylor. No one was openly gay there, at least in the law school, and it really didn't occur to me that some of my students might be hiding that part of their lives. Baylor was focused on trial law and advocacy, and the personal narratives of faculty or students rarely became important. I was hired at Baylor, served there for ten years, and departed for St. Thomas without ever having challenged the open discrimination of the school against people like my friends. Others did, though—Bob Baird, a philosophy professor, was especially brave in this way. His daughter, Katherine Baird Darmer, later became a key force pushing me toward honesty on this issue. My inaction while I was at Baylor was a failing, and one that was inconsistent with my claim to be progressive and inclusive.

When I got to St. Thomas, something remarkable happened. Not long after I started, a student in my class and I went to a local restaurant for lunch so that we could talk about his job search. He was looking for a position doing civil rights work. I noted that this was unusual for a white man, and he shrugged and said, "Well, I'm gay."

Quickly I looked behind me to make sure that no one had heard him say that. At Baylor, it was something that a person would keep as a deep secret and would never mention so casually. I needn't have worried. As I found out later, two of my colleagues on the faculty were openly gay; there was a Lesbian, Gay, Bisexual, and Transgender (LGBT) support group at the law school; and my administrative assistant was gay and kept a picture of his boyfriend on top of his desk. It turned out that a school could both have a religious identity *and* treat gay men and lesbians fairly.

It shook me as I began to think through what I had been a party to at Baylor. A friend suggested I look up some videos made for Dan Savage's *It Gets Better* project, in which LGBT adults describe how their lives turned out well despite prejudice. The first one I pulled up was by Randy Roberts Potts, the gay grandson of televangelist Oral Roberts. I watched it twice; I pulled my shades; and I cried.

The next week, in October 2010, I wrote a piece for the *Huffington Post* titled "Repentance of an Anti-Gay Bigot." It ran on the front page of the site, and quickly I heard from dozens of people, some supportive and others hostile. Among the messages were several from my former students at Baylor. They followed a common pattern, beginning with a statement expressing a simple fact: "Professor Osler, I was your student at Baylor, and I'm gay." From there, many of them told me what it had meant to hide their true selves in law school. One former student listed each of the things that had come with the rules of Baylor: the loss of a long-term relationship, physical illness, and a grade spiral from As to Ds. I was heartbroken.

One of those notes was from Joy Tull. I remembered her, of course; she is one of the most memorable people I have ever met. In class, she was one of the students who challenged me on facts that seemed out of place (that happens in sentencing law) and often raised the question that others were thinking. She chased me down after class, too. Sometimes, it was to follow up on a class discussion while at other times she just wanted to critique my clothes. She was particularly critical of my shoes; she retains a fervent hatred for L. L. Bean Boat-Mocs. More important, Joy was a force to be reckoned with because of her talents in the courtroom. She had a winning combination of intelligence and competitiveness, along with a Texan's natural ability to relate to a wide variety of people in the jury or the witness box. In courtroom exercises in my class, she was a natural star. Her note came as a surprise.

"Really?" Joy asked me later. "The deep voice, awesome at softball, never had a boyfriend? Really, you didn't know?"

But I hadn't. Once I knew, though, I realized why law school had been hard for someone whose talents were so well suited to the profession. She was hiding, and Joy does not possess the quiet reserve that makes hiding easy. She was constructed to live life out loud.

Once we were reconnected, I determined not to let Joy go again. When I was in Dallas for work, I stopped in for lunch with Joy and her then-girlfriend. We ate outside at a burger place, and Joy was at home in a way I had not seen before. Remembering her talents in the courtroom, I asked if she would be interested in helping me prosecute Jesus. She responded with enthusiasm, an excitement I hadn't expected.

Over time, I began to see the multiple sources of that enthusiasm. One was the fact that she could prosecute Jesus; she was no longer a believer and deeply resented the way in which she had been hurt and rejected by others, all in the name of Jesus. Her church and family had spent years teaching that what she was—a lesbian—was sinful and wrong because their ironclad faith and the words of their pastors demanded that view. When we later went to battle in the courtroom side by side, I was deeply troubled by the project of making an argument against Christ, but Joy reveled in it. She was, in a way, getting back at her bully.

It was also a distraction from her job as an associate at a large, Dallas law firm, a lucrative but soul-sucking vocation. Like many of my other most-talented students, Joy took the expected path of working for a large firm. And like many of those students, it made her miserable. In part their misery came from the long hours and grumpy bosses, but there was something deeper, too. They were my favorite students, usually, because they had a deep spirituality and sense of morality. At a law firm, their vocation, the project of their days, was fundamentally amoral—a law firm will take the paying client who comes in the door, and which side they represent often depends on who happened to hire them first. These best and brightest found work taking orders from a senior associate who took orders from a partner who took orders from a client who often was motivated by nothing more than the hope that he or she could win some money by going to court. When these former students checked in with me, I could often hear despair in their voices.

Joy wanted to do something with me that would take her away from those long days. Jeanne wanted to end the death penalty. Sara wanted to work with Jeanne. I was now driving a bus that was full of people who were often more emotionally committed to the project than I was. That's how we all ended up in Chicago on a January day in 2012—Jeanne, Joy, Sara, Phil Steger, and (most reluctant of all) me. It had been Jeanne's idea that we do the trial at her downtown Presbyterian church prior to a swing south to Tennessee, Oklahoma, and Virginia.

There was also a new face with our group. Joshua Rofe was a filmmaker from Los Angeles who was interested in documenting the project, and we welcomed him in. He was a wiry Brooklyn-to-L.A. transplant who had gotten to know Jeanne in the course of working on a film about the sentence of life without parole for juvenile offenders (a film that he later edited to completely eliminate her interviews while keeping those of Jeanne's family members who support that sentence). He was different from the rest of us—the only one not from the middle of the country, and his edginess provided an intriguing contrast. I didn't quite trust him, though, and this distrust proved correct in the end.

Josh's plan was to build a film around a single staging of the trial. Jeanne (a native Oklahoman) had already set up a performance at Crossings, a nondenominational megachurch in Oklahoma City. Josh was excited about the possibility of filming it; his hope was to capture it the same way that NFL films memorialize a classic football game. There would be shots of the crowds gathering, the players preparing, all building up to the event itself. It was a compelling idea.

In a way, there were three new characters in the drama. Josh was one, and there was already a new dynamic at play because it was the first time that Joy would try the case with us. The third character was the city of Chicago itself. To non-Chicagoan Midwesterners like Sara, Phil, and me, Chicago is the ultimate big city of the plains—full of danger and wonder that far exceeded what we knew in Minneapolis. I still walk down Michigan Avenue with a certain sense of awe at the scope of the city and its hurly-burly pace.

Fourth Church itself fits this sense of the grand. It is a cathedral, bigger than many of the grand cathedrals of Europe, situated on perhaps the best real estate in Chicago—directly on Michigan Avenue across from the John Hancock Building and Water Tower Place. It fronts the street with tall, imposing doors and backs up to a gorgeous community center that melds into the city seamlessly. It is not unusual to find the back of the church full of tourists, gawking at the vaulted ceiling and the remarkable sense of space. It was all a bit overwhelming.

With the addition of Josh we now had a new challenge as well: helping to raise money to support his documentary. Almost immediately after everyone met on the curb by a bustling Michigan Avenue hotel, we piled into a car and drove to a fund-raiser generously held by a Fourth Church member and friend of Jeanne's. Not ten minutes after introductions we were clamoring out of a car like a family after a long road trip, grousing about being hungry, wanting to order pizza, and trying to decide whether we needed to change clothes.

We went upstairs to a light-filled apartment that was all yellows. The hosts were generous and accommodating, and the gorgeous spread of food drove thoughts of Chicago pizza from our minds. People were coming to this apartment to support the trial of Christ and have some small part in opposing the death penalty. The party felt like the launch of our ship, the bottle broken on the bow. Outside the window, a crystal-clear January day revealed the broad sweep of Lakeshore Drive as it traced the icy shore of Lake Michigan.

Once everyone at the party had gotten themselves a drink, Jeanne spoke. These were her people: her friends from the North Shore, stalwarts of the church, people from the courthouse, and even her own elegant, attentive mother. As a veteran of such situations, Jeanne spoke compellingly and simply, describing our run-up to engaging the Southern states of Oklahoma and Tennessee. The crowd was captivated by Jeanne's combination of steel-nerved trial lawyer and soprano storyteller. Joshua followed, looking the very image of a young filmmaker in jeans and a casual buttoned shirt. Checks were written.

Jeanne has a long history at Fourth Presbyterian: She sang in the choir for over two decades, served on the church's governing board twice, and even appeared and sang in the movie *My Best Friend's Wedding* with Julia Roberts and Cameron Diaz in a scene at the church (a stint for which she still gets residual checks). It wasn't new to me, either. In the summer of 1988 I lived nearby while working a summer job during law school and attended services there several times. On one of those visits, on a steaming summer day in July, I had seen something that had come to define the church in my mind. Sitting in front of me, hip to hip, were a mother and her young daughter. The girl was fidgety, and when the sermon began, the mother slipped her a pad of paper and a pencil. She suddenly became attentive, leaning forward and marking down counting marks frequently, four vertical lines crossed with a diagonal to make sets of five.

Fascinated by this process, I tried to guess what, exactly, she was counting. Her marks piled up—eleven, twelve, thirteen. Toward the end of the sermon, I finally cracked the code. She was counting how many times the minister, John Buchanan, used the word *love*. It is a metric I still value when writing or listening to a sermon.

The trial was scheduled for early afternoon, after the morning services and before the 4:00 p.m. "jazz vespers." We had prepared our witnesses and were now just awaiting the arrival of the judge. For the first time, we would have an actual Cook County trial judge, Larry Axelrood, preside over the trial. Jeanne Bishop regularly tried cases before Judge Axelrood, so this magnified her home-field advantage.

That familiarity was evident as we settled in for the performance. A line of people came forward to embrace Jeanne, while Joy and I huddled over our notes. At every turn, Joy had an idea grounded in both her remarkable knowledge of Scriptures and her desire to show the dangers of Christ. By the time we were done talking, my pad was covered with red marks deleting passive statements and adding new attacks. When we were done and in agreement, she turned and looked me in the eye. "Hey, Osler," she intoned, "does my hair look good?" It did.

It was time to begin, and Joy took the stage at the front of the cathedral to give our opening statement. The minute she began, I saw for the first time two of her greatest courtroom strengths: a warm, welcoming smile and a soft Texas accent. Both defused the sharp edge of our presentation. If you are asking a group of Christians to kill Jesus, tone matters.

Even though I was mindful of that necessary tone, I was determined to follow my revised notes and be more aggressive this time around in advancing evidence and making my arguments. My strategy, again, was to emphasize how dangerous Jesus was to the very foundations of society: family, economy, and government. In the past, I had been too passive in relating the challenge Jesus presented to society.

Phil appeared again as Peter and had the advantage of knowing where I was going. In Minneapolis, for example, I had stumped him on redirect with the fact that he had taken the witness oath. This was in violation of Jesus' teaching—Christ directed his followers, " 'Do not swear at all, either by heaven, for it is the throne of God, or by the earth, for it is his footstool. . . . Let your word be "Yes, Yes," or "No, No"; anything more than this comes from the evil one' " (Matt. 5:34–37). This time around, Phil refused to take the oath, to the bemusement of Judge Axelrood, who shrugged.

One of the stipulations we had was that Peter was a hostile witness, and thus I could treat him as if on cross-examination, using leading questions. This time I asked more specifically about the things Jesus had taught, focusing especially on the threat those teachings presented to families. Jesus had forsaken a family himself and pulled his followers away from their own families. When his mother and brothers came to see him, he turned them away, saying that those traveling with him were his true family. More troubling, he taught that his own goal was to

> "set a man against his father,
> and a daughter against her mother,
> . . . .
> and one's foes will be members of one's own household."
> (Matt. 10:35–36)

As I pressed Phil on these statements, I saw the discomfort of some in our audience. We want Christianity to affirm what is familiar to us, and my attack on Jesus' teachings contradicted those expectations.

Jeanne and Sara countered on cross-examination, turning Peter to Jesus' actions in healing people and showing kindness to the outcasts in society. As before, Phil reacted with great enthusiasm, describing each event in loving detail.

The year before in Minneapolis, the young man who acted as the rich young ruler was the perfect combination of shiny-suited obliviousness and a too-dark tan; nobody roots for that guy. At Fourth Church, though, the rich young ruler was a handsome young man in unassuming clothes who genuinely came off as though all he wanted to do was please God, and that guy (pointing his thumb at Jesus) told him that because he wouldn't get rid of his wealth, a camel had a better chance of passing through the eye of a needle than he had of getting into heaven. Jesus told him to destroy his life in order to follow God's truth (see Luke 18:18–25). His life looked a lot like many of the lives of the affluent jurors seated before us. By the prosecution's view, Jesus was telling people to dismantle the economic vitality of civilization. Jeanne cross-examined the rich young ruler, and he admitted that Jesus didn't tell everyone to get rid of their wealth, just him. While this took a bit of the sting away, we could all feel how troubling his testimony had been to the jury, some of whom had more in common with this witness than any other.

As in Richmond, the theme of slavery came into play. Jeanne had called two witnesses, a Roman centurion (whose slave had been healed by Jesus, Luke 7:2–10) and Malchus, the slave who had his ear cut off by Peter at the time of Jesus' arrest (Luke 22:49–51). On cross-examination, Joy and I brought forth a central point—that though Jesus had healed each of these slaves, he had not freed them.

A church member, Ed Miller, played the role of Malchus. Like our other witnesses thus far (in a streak that was about to end), Ed was remarkably knowledgeable about the Gospels and his character. This led to a singularly dramatic moment, perhaps the most dramatic in our trials to that point. Malchus was not only a slave; the book of John tells us that he was the property of Caiaphas—that is, he was the property of the prosecutor of Jesus . . . me. When Ed took the stand and received the oath, he seemed an unassuming character in the drama. That changed quickly. As soon as he sat down, I asked him, "You are a slave, aren't you?"

He looked a little downcast. "Yes, I am," he replied.

With a cruel edge in my voice, I asked him a leading question (as allowed on cross-examination): "In fact you are *my* slave, right?"

He looked down, defeated and obedient. "Yes, master," he said in a low voice.

In the audience, there was a shocked stillness. A few people were rustling through the pew Bibles, trying to verify this account. I continued my interrogation. "And when he healed you, when the defendant healed your ear, you came back to my service, didn't you?"

"Yes."

"And when I tell you to come, you come, and when I tell you to go, you go, and if I decide you should be beaten or die, that is my right?"

He nodded, still looking down. Quietly he answered, "Yes."

There was something inside me that I had never felt, something darker than I had known in my previous experiences with the trial. For that bare moment I *was* Caiaphas and felt the surge of power that comes with having dominion, possession, ownership, of another person. It was an overwhelming and terrible thing but palpable, real. I reached for a note and saw Sara looking at me, aghast.

By closing arguments we were in a real fight. In her turn, Jeanne argued in her calm, strong voice for Jesus to get the same mercy he had offered to others. When she was done, I jumped out of my seat for rebuttal, saying, "Mercy!!?!? You call leaving a slave a slave mercy!!?!" As we sat and waited through their thirty minutes of deliberations, no one felt confident in the outcome of the juries. The groups, though, coalesced quickly and soon entered into heated debates. As we saw everywhere else, the idea of allowing the audience to continue the conversation led to a remarkable commitment to the project.

In the end, we lost again; every ballot was for the defense. As the verdicts came in, read one by one by Judge Axelrood, I became myself again; I stopped being Caiaphas. As I did, there was a wave of emotional exhaustion and repulsion that overwhelmed all else. Becoming Caiaphas was more than I had bargained for—the story had carried me someplace unexpected and hard, carried me there as swiftly as a wild horse carries a rider to places unknown. It was deeply unsettling. At dinner after the trial, I knew that I was distant and troubled, even as the others laughed and recounted the vivid moments of the day. I had thought that I was writing the story of this trial, controlling its trajectory, but here in Chicago I began to understand that I might be wrong.

Sara Sommervold, Jeanne Bishop, Sara's husband Scott,
and Joy Tull in Cambridge
(photo courtesy of Mark Osler; used by permission)

Chapter 4

Cambridge, Massachusetts

Just three weeks after the adventure in Chicago, the full cast was to perform the trial at the Episcopal Divinity School (EDS) in Cambridge, Massachusetts. EDS is an unusual and very liberal institution; they were not the people who supported the death penalty. Rather than advocacy, this was another test run before we returned to the South, in front of people who largely agreed with us.

My goal was to learn (and perhaps teach) something about advocacy and practice the trial in front of a smart, critical audience. In the end, that goal was achieved, though the real drama was within my own team. By the time we left Boston with our next destinations in the South, I knew that the trial was turning out to be changing and challenging *us* in a more obvious way than it was changing and challenging our audiences. I was becoming more conflicted; Sara was getting drawn deeper into questions of faith; and Jeanne was being pulled into her own forgiveness narrative with her sister's killer. Joy, though, was about to face a completely different inner (and, as it turned out, outer) conflict.

Joy grew up in a very defined brand of American Christianity. Her family was not the stereotype of hard-core evangelicals. Her mother is a medical doctor, and her father is a graduate of Macalester College, the renowned liberal arts school in St. Paul, known for its liberal student body. These facts aside, they raised Joy in a strict fundamentalist household and sent her off to college at Southwest Assemblies of God University in Waxahachie, Texas, whose "mission and core values" includes "personal edification through speaking in tongues in private prayer" according to its Web site.

Joy had only partly left that world behind. Though she found a girlfriend and a community in Dallas, it was clear that being gay had to be a secret at her Dallas law firm. Not that it was a well-kept secret—Joy couldn't help but notice the disapproval of some of the partners. She was good at her work, but it did not feed her truer needs. She is someone who is at her best when she feels a passion for the side she is on, and she had little passion for the interests of the corporations her firm represented. It is a pattern I have seen again and again with my best students: the very thing, the passion, that made them great advocates becomes their undoing when they take a job that is amoral at best, often representing rich entities when they are sued by working people.

Having come out (mostly) as a lesbian and been rejected by much of the world that had raised her, Joy was now angry with God and with the self-appointed messengers of God who had taught her the shape and contours of faith and the world. The narrowness and harsh outlook of her family and church led Joy to see Christianity with stark, sure boundaries—a line she once was inside of and now had busted through to the outside. It was that bright line that formed her language about faith, which often centered on "real" churches— those that only had Communion once a month, centered their rhetoric on sin, and demonized people like Joy.

Episcopal Divinity School, as I knew, was the opposite of what Joy considered a "real" church institution. It trains ministers for both the Episcopal church and for Metropolitan Community Churches, a denomination with a specific and affirming outreach to gay, lesbian, bisexual, and transgendered people. St. John's Memorial Chapel, on the EDS campus, has hosted same-sex weddings since 1995, and the dean at that time, Katherine Ragsdale, was a lesbian, pro-choice activist. In other words, EDS was full of people like Joy. I was bringing her into something that did not, could not, exist in her world—a church that did not reject her. Much as I hoped that bringing the faith of Christians into juxtaposition with their support of the death penalty might create dissonance, I suspected that bringing Joy to a church that was not a "real" church in her mind would create an inner conflict. I was more right than I could know. First, though, we had some meetings and a party.

I had gotten to Boston before the others, in part to meet with Reginald Dwayne Betts, a poet who held a fellowship at Harvard. He was working on a book of poems about crack (since released as *Bastards of the Reagan Era*)[1] and wanted to talk to me about my work on both sides of that issue—first as a prosecutor imposing harsh laws and then as an advocate for reform. I visited him in his comfortable office in the Radcliffe quad and found his work fascinating. He had come to Harvard through an unorthodox route; he was arrested at age sixteen for carjacking, was sentenced as an adult, and spent eight years in prison. It was there that he began writing poetry, and after earning a degree at the University of Maryland, he began a remarkable career as a writer. Later in the week, I was crossing a street with Jeanne Bishop after a prep session at EDS, and Dwayne was coming the other way. He slowed as we approached. I thought it was to greet me but then realized it was Jeanne that he was focused on. In the middle of Garden Street off of Cambridge Common, the three of us stopped in our tracks.

"Jeanne Bishop," Dwayne said flatly.

"Dwayne," Jeanne replied, nodding coolly before stepping past him.

I was stunned to find that they knew each other. It was an emotionally freighted exchange reminiscent of Seinfeld/Newman encounters on the *Seinfeld* show, and I was dying to know the backstory. As it turned out, it struck at an internal conflict as deep as Joy's—Jeanne had been Dwayne's opponent in a fierce law-school-hosted debate over the sentence of life without parole for juveniles. Dwayne, convicted at sixteen, thought the sentence inhumane. Jeanne, who lost her sister to a sixteen-year-old with a gun, disagreed. Now, though, cracks were showing in Jeanne's resolve on the issue, but she was not showing that to her old opponent.

As we walked away, I looked at Jeanne. "You know each other."

She nodded and looked over her shoulder at where Dwayne had been. "It was a while ago." She was quiet for a minute and then continued. "I don't think I was fair to him back then." Then we walked in silence. She looked lost in thought.

---

1. Reginald Dwayne Betts, *Bastards of the Reagan Era* (New York: Four Way Books, 2015).

It was Super Bowl Sunday—the Giants versus Boston's beloved Patriots. While the rest of us were staying at the Sheraton Commander near Harvard and EDS, Jeanne had booked herself at a bed-and-breakfast, in a little house tucked away from the street. At the appointed hour we all arrived at her little bungalow as the town buzzed around us, anticipating the game. Despite the conflicts each of us had brought with us, we put on a good party. Jeanne and Joy sang church-camp songs, and I ran out for pizza and beer. When the Patriots made a first down, you could hear the town react—horns would honk, and shouts could be heard through the shut windows. Boston is like that.

Then it was the halftime show, which featured Madonna. With the help of a marching band, a lengthy series of special appearances by A-list guests like CeeLo Green and Nicki Minaj, and a brief but spectacular Roman theme, Madonna's show was an overloaded flaming boat full of fireworks. The end was equally over the top: the stadium went black for a moment, the photo opposite of the tumult of the preceding twelve minutes, and then the words "World Peace" appeared, utterly without context and to a frantic chorus of applause. Somehow, there was something utterly ridiculous and thrilling about that, and we laughed ourselves hoarse. It may have been because we were attempting to make a political point with excruciating subtlety and layers of subtext, and Madonna was taking an even broader point and using it as a commercialized cudgel. Someone said, "Can't we just do *that*?"

Walking into the cold night air, I looked down Concord Avenue toward Harvard Law School. I lived in Cambridge, not far from that spot, when I chose to go to Yale for law school. I remember the moment well—standing before a bulletin board in Pound Hall at Harvard Law, looking at the fascinating posters for lectures, and deciding that I would go to Yale and then someday come back to that spot to see a poster with my name on it. Exactly that had happened three years before and twice since then, so as I stood in that cold air with my friends, it seemed that I had made the right choice. Yale Law was a ticket to the chance I now had, a chit to cash in when I asked schools and churches to let us be heard.

The next morning, we gathered at the divinity school to begin plotting out the trial. We met Dean Ragsdale and some of the staff who would be helping us. Almost as soon as we entered the building, Joy seemed tense and cautious. As she wrote to me later, it was because of the combination of Christianity and lesbians: "There were lesbians. Everywhere. My impeccable gaydar is the result of trying to find other women to connect with romantically while being raised in church and attending Bible College. If gaydar were a superpower, Bible College would be the planet Superman is from. And my gaydar was hopping."

Joy's anxiety perplexed me. I had expected that what would be hard for her would be going to a place like her home church in San Antonio, where hostility to gay men and lesbians was a part of the culture. At EDS, where her sexual identity was accepted and embraced, I expected her to feel at home. That failed expectation reflected how much I had to learn.

Jeanne and I carefully plotted out how we would transform the classroom we were led to into a courtroom, a task that can be tricky. There must be sight lines between the witness and the judge, lawyers, and podium, for example. Over time we would do the trial in church sanctuaries, classrooms, lecture halls, and foyers, and each presented a different challenge. In this room, the primary challenge would be working in such a small space, so we moved tables out to the corners of the room and replaced comfortable chairs with smaller ones.

As we did so, I gauged the mood of my collaborators. Jeanne was confident but cautious while Joy was clearly unsettled by this new mix of Christianity and LGBT celebration, which challenged a core tenet of her upbringing: that you could either be gay or Christian, but you couldn't be both. It was Sara who seemed most comfortable in this unusual place. The combination of the liturgy and look of old-school church with progressive theology was precisely what she had sought out in her adult life as an Episcopalian. Sara was always gracious and a master of social situations, but here she was best situated to take the lead and did so. She and Dean Ragsdale clearly took to each other immediately as we toured the facility, which is on the fringe of the Harvard University campus. One of Sara's gifts is a warm, welcoming laugh, and it was often heard as we walked up the stone steps of the school.

After setting up the room for the trial, we walked over to a service in St. John's Chapel on the EDS campus. Walking into the church, we were handed bulletins, an event that sent Joy into a spiral of decrying this lesbian-led service as something other than a "real church." I later asked her what she was thinking as we walked in, and she replied with vivid detail:

> The church appeared to be 50 percent lesbian. I thought I missed something; churches don't have lesbians. And they certainly aren't half queer. Then service started, and they gave a lesbian in a robe an award for her service with the homeless. Yup, not a real church. Real churches don't give out awards. You work really hard at not sinning, and no one gives you awards because you don't get awards for doing what you're supposed to do. Notably the difference between "not sinning" and how this church clearly defined "being a Christian" are vast. It's amazing in retrospect, but caring for the homeless is not "not sinning" and therefore not the focus of the places I grew up. Not listening to secular music, not drinking, not having sex before you're married, not reading Harry Potter books or watching Captain Planet—those were the things we put our energy into. Caring for the poor, immigrants, and single mothers didn't make the list. We were too busy trying not to sin.

When Joy explained all this to me, I finally understood something I had missed: the anger that some conservative Christians felt toward the idea of "social justice." Her understanding of the faith was sometimes startling, even though she was no longer a believer. Time and again, Jeanne would quote the Bible, and Joy would quickly remind her of the verse immediately before or after the section Jeanne had cited.

Sitting next to Joy in the pew was a trial in itself. Every few seconds, she would poke me in the side to complain about the service or the printed program. According to Joy, the program was another sign that this wasn't a "real" church because the cover featured the blessing "Welcome one and all, you are welcome to find peace here" rather than a photo of the church. Apparently, peace was not to be my fate, at least that morning. Her questions intensified as Communion approached. Another poke in the ribs. "It's not going to be real wine. Grape juice, right? Right?"

I might be a new Episcopalian, but I wasn't that new. "No, real wine," I told her while swatting away her still-poking finger. She threw her hands in the air and muttered about the lesbians again.

A few moments later, though, my favorite unbeliever was kneeling next to me, taking the bread and wine from a woman in white robes. She was faking it, I suppose, but I wasn't, and there was a moment of transcendence as the priest put the host gently in my cupped hands, looked in my eyes, and said, "The bread of life." Next, she did the same for Joy, who took and ate.

I loved her for that, for kneeling with me even as she suffered such inner tumult. It was an act of grace I won't forget. In large measure, she wasn't wrong to feel the jarring disjuncture between this setting and the larger churches of her youth. I remembered what had happened when I had written a piece for CNN titled "The Christian Case for Gay Marriage." It received over fifteen thousand comments on the Web site, and dozens of people e-mailed me their views directly. The first of these arrived just moments after the story posted online, and the message contained only one word: "Idiot!" That was tame compared to scores of others, most of which let me know that I was going to hell and some of which added the oddly specific point that I was to be cast into a lake of burning sulfur. Nearly all these people self-identified as Christians and pointed to Christianity as the source of their opposition to my view. In saying that most Christians were hostile to people like her, Joy was probably right.

All these things were on my mind as I explored this unusual outpost of the faith. After the service, I headed off to meetings at Harvard Law while Sara, Jeanne, and Joy went their own ways. There was a plan to all reconvene that evening at Legal Seafood, a Boston institution with a branch just off the Harvard campus.

It was a wonderful afternoon, discussing the state of sentencing with one of my academic heroes, Harvard professor and former federal judge Nancy Gertner. Judge Gertner is one of those rare people whose influence is out of proportion to her time with me— much of what I have learned from her came from reading her opinions (which I did regularly while she was on the bench). I first met her in 2000, when my sentencing mentor at Yale Law, Dan Freed, invited me back to the Sentencing Workshop class I had been a part of when I was a third-year law student. At that point, Prof. Freed was co-teaching it with Judge Gertner. At my very first meeting, we had a spirited argument. Afterward, I heard her say to Yale Professor Kate Stith, "It's the reasonable-sounding prosecutors who give you the most trouble." I took it as a compliment; at least I sounded reasonable.

On this afternoon, Judge Gertner showed me into her office; it was not only full of the usual awards, photos, and books, but there was also a stack of brown boxes piled high against the wall. Looking at the stack with sadness, she said, "You know what that is, right?"

I didn't and shook my head, a little confused.

"Those are Dan's papers," she said, and so they were. Professor Freed had died the previous year, leaving behind a legion of "Freedians," a group of judges, academics, and practitioners who had been marked by his conviction that sentencing was important, that the guidelines had failed, and that hard work and study were needed to make things right. I was, and am, a Freedian. Given that legacy, it was heartbreaking to learn that Yale Law had declined to catalog Professor Freed's papers, allowing only that Judge Gertner would be able to cart them away and try to preserve them. "This," I thought, "is what was left of his work" before realizing how wrong I was. What was left of his work was also within me, within Judge Gertner, and within the others he had inspired to twine their vocations around the issues of sentencing and incarceration.

Meanwhile, Joy and Sara had spent the afternoon hashing things out at a hotel bar. Jeanne and I met up at the restaurant at the appointed time. I was a little dejected; seeing my mentor's work piled up in boxes was a gut punch. With no sign of Joy and Sara, we got a table for four and ordered an appetizer. The restaurant was quiet and hushed—Monday is not a busy night, even in bustling Cambridge. There was one couple there in the adjacent booth, with the look of Harvard graduate students on a second date. While I was quiet with that lingering sadness, Jeanne was excited to have seen her friend Mary Pike, who was to serve as the judge at our trial the next day. As she was describing her history with Mary, a tale that involved the Irish Republican Army, the Supreme Court, and various levels of international intrigue, Joy and Sara arrived.

It's hard to understate the alarming appearance they made, like firemen rushing into a building on fire. They located us in our quiet corner next to the graduate students and blustered over. On the way, even before finding the table, Joy corralled a startled waiter and ordered another drink. It was clear that Joy was ready to share her views. Sara leaned over conspiratorially and in the kind of stage whisper that actresses like her have perfected, she murmured, "Get ready." The eruption began just as the drink arrived. Joy had a full head of steam and no volume control. Her rage was unmitigated, remarkable, and overwhelming. Part of what sparked her was the fact that I have described myself as an evangelical Christian.

Joy looked me square in the eye and started in. What had probably been a measured conversation with Sara throughout the afternoon was now Joy yelling at the idea of God—a God that causes suffering, if he really does create all reality; a God that does nothing in a world that supports the death penalty, homophobia, and racism. She was furious at the idea of a God that sends people to hell for drinking, dancing, and being gay. "Real Christians," she told us, "would call that service we went to today a blasphemous abomination." In short, she was telling us, and the whole restaurant, why evangelicals are wrong and how they wouldn't see me or Jeanne or Sara as real Christians, and that we weren't evangelicals. "Real Christians"—the evangelicals—were the ones who rejected her and people like her. We couldn't be evangelical Christians, or she would have to hate us, too.

Jeanne and I had known this would come, but it was still hard to hear; Joy's pain was so clear and real. After a moment to catch her breath and rub away her first tear, Joy continued, "My parents are really sad that I'm going to hell 'cause I'm gay. My mom turned to me last weekend and said, 'I'm just sorry you're going to hell. Would you like some cake?'" Jeanne moved to hug her, but Joy shrugged her off as the couple behind her looked increasingly uncomfortable.

She looked straight at me. "There is some kid in India starving to death right now, and God just says, 'Fuck you, starving kid'? That same God let me grow up in a community claiming to represent him, and didn't stop them. That's the God you believe in? The one who tells that kid and lets others tell me, 'Fuck you, I hate you'?" She was crying, yelling, anguished. At the heart of her anguish was a faith—an evangelical Christianity—that focused on sin rather than love.

I was stopped cold, not so much by her raw emotion but by the truth in what she said. Behind her, the graduate students called for the check. There was nothing to say, no explanation to give, and neither Jeanne nor I tried. If we began this project to find challenge and truth, we had found it. There was an ineffable beauty to Joy's rage, an undeniable, heart-stopping rawness. We would never forget what we now call the Loud Dinner.

I have lived a life full of intense moments. I have met with presidents, prosecuted crack dealers, caught a shark, climbed mountains, and debated policy with Jeffery Toobin on CNN. No moment, though, equals that one as an eruption of raw truth or brutal epiphany. It wasn't striking because Joy was loud but because she was right, and the pain inside her was strong proof of what she asserted. She was putting before me something at a very primal level that I had never felt. As advocacy, it was the best I have yet seen. We all were changed.

Of course, there was a next morning. I asked everyone to meet in the lobby of the Sheraton Commander to go over our examinations and arguments to make sure we were on track. Sara seemed unscathed, but Joy looked as if she might not survive. As became our custom, for our final preparation we split up into our respective teams. Sara and Jeanne went to a coffee shop, and Joy and I stayed at the hotel.

It was the first time Sara and Joy would be handling the opening statements in the trial, and we wanted to be sure that they were ready. Joy, even in her state, was still a natural litigator, and as she laid out her opening, I could see it was cut to Baylor Law's strict specifications. After a few run-throughs, I let her go find a cheeseburger.

As I watched Joy head out, I sat back and recalled the prior evening. I was like a boxer who had been hit hard and was just getting up off the mat. Perhaps Joy and Madonna were right; my advocacy of subtlety and juxtaposition might be inadequate, even silly, in a world of rank injustice. I could tell that Sara, too, was moved both by Joy and by Jeanne's gradual revealing of her own beliefs. Back at school, Sara would often recount in precise detail the stories that Jeanne had told about prison wardens and robberies and the gritty realities of courts in Chicago.

That evening, it was a remarkable setting. The trial at the divinity school drew an intriguing group of students and faculty jammed into the small room. I liked that; I prefer to be within a few feet of my audience, to be able to see their eyes and movements, to sense the intimacy of a moment when a story unfolds that overlaps with their own.

Two people in the audience saw the case with a deep connection. Like Jeanne, they had lost family members to murder and knew her from their common campaign against the death penalty. Bob Curley had lost his son to a gruesome crime, and Renny Cushing suffered loss of his family in two separate murders. Both were Jeanne's collaborators in a world-spanning project to challenge the death penalty.

Bob Curley is a Cambridge firefighter with dark eyes, a thick Boston accent ("shaht" for "short" and "cahner" for "corner") and a woeful past. In 1997, Bob's ten-year-old son Jeffrey had been abducted and murdered by two pedophiles. They lured Jeffrey into a car with the promise of a bicycle. They demanded sex in exchange, which the boy refused. As he struggled to fight them off, the killers smothered the boy with a gasoline-soaked rag. They took the murdered child to another location, where they stripped him and repeatedly sodomized the boy's dead body. When they were done, they stuffed Jeffrey's body into a plastic container and dumped it into the Great Works River.

At the time of Jeffrey's murder, Massachusetts did not have a death penalty. Bob joined efforts to have the death penalty restored for certain crimes, including the rape and murder of a child under the age of fourteen. Over time, though, Bob changed his mind about the death penalty—in no small part because of an encounter he had with two other men near his age who had also suffered the tragedy of murder: Renny Cushing and Bud Welch.

The three men met on a television talk show in Boston where they had been invited to discuss the death-penalty-reinstatement debate in Massachusetts. Bob was to be the spokesman on the pro-death-penalty side; Renny and Bud were on the side of death-penalty abolition. Renny had lost his father to murder by an off-duty policeman in Hampton, New Hampshire, in 1988. The officer shot the senior Cushing to death in front of his wife, Marie, on the front steps of his home. Bud Welch's only daughter, Julie Marie, had been killed in the Oklahoma City bombing perpetrated by Timothy McVeigh in 1995.

Bob at first didn't want to appear on the show, concerned that Cushing and Welch would villify him for his pro–death-penalty position. Instead, the two men affirmed his grief, understood his rage, and defended on the program Curley's right to his position. The men shared a ride back to Cambridge after the show and parted as friends. Over time, Bob Curley changed his mind about the death penalty, partly because of the flaws he saw in the criminal justice system that tried the two men who killed Jeffrey and partly because he didn't want Jeffrey's memorial to be renewed executions. Instead, Curley works to protect child safety.

Cushing, unbelievably, had lost not one but two family members to murder, years apart. On March 28, 2011, Cushing's brother-in-law Stephen McRedmond was shot to death on the steps of his Nashville home by his twenty-five-year-old nephew, Brendan McRedmond, who then took his own life. A crime eerily similar to the one that took the life of Renny's father, the murder occurred on the steps of Stephen's home, in front of his spouse. That spouse was Renny Cushing's brother, Matthew.

Renny had performed the wedding of the couple, who had been together for thirty-five years, not long before in the state of New Hampshire, where Renny is a state representative. New Hampshire had recently passed a law permitting same-sex marriage, a bill that Renny had lobbied for strenuously. Matthew and Stephen's wedding was a joyous occasion, particularly for Marie Cushing, Matthew and Renny's elderly mom, who rejoiced to see the last of her eight children walk down the aisle.

On March 31, 2011, Renny presided again, over a crowd gathered to celebrate the life and mourn the death of his brother-in-law Stephen. The casket lay under a huge, spreading tree on the banks of a wide, rushing creek, just steps from the home Stephen and Matthew so lovingly built and shared.

Nor were Renny and Bob the only ones in the room with deep connections to Jeanne. Our judge that night was Mary Pike. Jeanne's activism in Northern Ireland had led her to Mary, the same activism that had led the FBI to Jeanne after Nancy's murder. Mary represented Joseph Doherty, a member of the IRA in his fight for political asylum in the United States. Doherty had escaped to Brooklyn from prison in Northern Ireland after he was convicted of killing a British soldier during a skirmish between the IR and a British patrol. He was arrested in New York in 1983, and Mary represented him in his political asylum case for the next nine years, arguing his case all the way to the U. S. Supreme Court. She's a force, with short-cropped gray hair, a small wiry frame, taut skin, and wide-open, attentive expression almost all the time. Not surprisingly she took her job as judge seriously, checking in with Jeanne to confirm that she had everything right before we started.

As Mary Pike debriefed with Jeanne, Sara and Joy were joshing around with the man playing Jesus, an EDS student in long, white robes. Joy had learned that a Texas accent was seen as charming in New England and used it to great effect as she tested his knowledge of the Bible against her own.

For the first time, our witnesses were unpredictable and varied widely in age, experience, and scriptural knowledge, or as we've come to think of them—"the facts." We all secretly (or not so secretly) wished we could conjure Phil Steger to act as Peter everywhere we go. The spirit that Phil brought to the role established Peter as the man Phil showed to us; when I thought of Peter, I saw Phil's face radiant with excitement.

Joy's adjustment to the realities and values of EDS was continuing. One of the witnesses she would prepare and examine in the early renditions of the trial was the rich young ruler, the one who seeks out Jesus only to be told that to achieve everlasting life he would have to sell all that he had and give it to the poor. The woman playing this role didn't have the biblical knowledge Joy did, which isn't surprising given Joy's upbringing. As we continued to perform the trial in churches and seminaries, it was rare to find anyone who had Joy's recall of Scripture. It was surprising to Joy, though. After she was done prepping the witness, she took me aside and confided with shock that this witness had been surprised to learn that the saying that it was as easy for the rich to achieve heaven as it was for a camel to pass through the eye of a needle was, in fact, from the Bible.

Sara and Joy opened the trial and were both true to form. Joy's Texas accent and Southern manners made the jury feel at ease, like she'd take care of them. Sara was measured but emotional, which gave the jury enough to make them think that maybe Joy was wrong. Jeanne and I once again hit an emotional pitch that led to my incredulous description of Christ's mercy, leaving me exhausted, as the trial always did.

I was still working out how to be a prosecutor in this setting. When I was an actual prosecutor back in Detroit, I had a particular style: dispassionate during the presentation of evidence, emotionally invested but not quite passionate during closing arguments, and finally emotional during rebuttal argument (which comprises just the last few minutes of a trial). That wasn't working for me in this setting, and over time I felt myself increasingly pulled toward a more consistent emotional edge.

There was one moment during the trial at EDS that has stayed with me, much as Joy's outburst of truth has. During closings, I was rolling through the evidence that had been presented and looked up at Renny Cushing, a man who had been victimized by not one but two murderers. He looked, as much as anything, sad. For a moment, I stumbled and fell silent. It is all tragedy, after all. Stepping into the well of the court now reminds me of that each time: that the events that draw us into those grand spaces are always wrapped up in loss and heartbreak and can rarely if ever offer hope.

The five of us stepped into the hall while the jury deliberated— we four litigators and the defendant, Jesus, in his long white robes. There is always a little silence in that moment, born of exhaustion and uncertainty. I feel it more than the others in our group, perhaps because I am the most uncertain.

Joy turned to our Jesus and said, "Sorry if they kill ya; I'm just doing my job."

Jesus didn't miss a beat. "Don't worry," he replied cheerily, "either way I'll be back in three days."

Thirty minutes into their deliberation the divinity school jury was unable to reach a verdict. These seminarians, who have dedicated themselves to a Christian life, couldn't decide if Jesus of Nazareth should be put to death. I think Sara was genuinely surprised. Perhaps coming from her own community it further complicated her faith. Whatever it was, Katherine Ragsdale, the dean of the divinity school, seemed to sense her unease.

Rev. Ragsdale cuts an impressive form. She's a towering figure with thick gray hair, an easy smile, and thoughtful eyes. She came over to tell us she thought the presentation was unique and powerful. The dean gave us encouragement: "You have something very important, and too rare—you have a narrative, a story that can deeply affect and move people. Often, over the course of my career, I've found myself speaking primarily to people who already agreed with me. The opportunity to reach diverse audiences with a compelling story—that's a rare and wonderful thing." I hoped that she was right.

Boston was hard for everyone. The Loud Dinner made clear the sacrifice that Joy was making to come on this journey, and we now got it. Going to Cambridge was not a part of our core mission—there was not a single death-penalty supporter in attendance—but it did expose us to a vital, fascinating community of faith. It wasn't just Joy who had never seen a place like it; none of us had.

The Episcopal Divinity School was a place seemingly constructed to convince people like Joy that they could be gay and Christian, that God's love was not defined by anyone but God. The fact that the bare existence of such a place challenged Joy so much was a stark lesson to me—about the often deep insights of the faithless, the terrifying power of both acceptance and rejection, and the complexities of definition.

Now we were ready to head south. Or so I thought.

Katherine Baird Darmer in her family room
(photo courtesy of Alice Baird; used by permission)

Chapter 5

Tennessee

*R*eturning to Minneapolis from Boston, I struggled with the eighty students taking Criminal Law—a large, first-year lecture class. It was just my second year of teaching the course, which was a different challenge from the seminars I was used to. It required a distinct and unfamiliar teaching style, the Socratic method. In between the trials in Boston and Tennessee, I hoped to focus on improving the class and my technique. I made little headway, though. The events in Boston, particularly the Loud Dinner, stuck with me and troubled me at several levels. What if Joy was right? Was my faith not "real," and was I wrong to describe myself as evangelical? There was a new focus to my doubts. Worse, a deep tragedy struck hard on February 17.

One thing already laid out in this book is that I value the collaboration of not only remarkable men like Randall O'Brien and Craig Anderson but also strong, smart women like Jeanne Bishop. One of those strong, smart women, and one of my primary influences as an academic, was Katherine Baird Darmer, a former prosecutor and a professor at Chapman Law School in California. Katherine was fortunate to be born from brilliance. Her parents, Bob and Alice Baird, are legends of the best kind at Baylor, where Bob was a philosophy professor. I remember once having dinner with the influential philosopher Dallas Willard, and despite my best efforts to raise other topics, Willard kept bringing the conversation back to Bob because of his deep respect for Professor Baird. It was Professor Baird who first introduced me to his daughter, Katherine, as he knew we had common interests. Once the introduction was made, I counted on

Katherine's advice over and over—not only about what to write or teach but about what was important.

One reason that Katherine provided such good advice to me was that our professional lives tracked each other nearly identically. We spoke the same language and knew the same body of truths. She went to Princeton undergrad and graduated from Columbia Law (as a Harlan Fisk Stone scholar) about the same time I graduated from Yale Law. Then we both clerked in federal court, worked for a big firm for three years, served as federal prosecutors from 1995–2000, and entered the academy in 2000, traveling parallel paths in lockstep, though we did not know each other yet. We both wrote about sentencing and (later) the civil rights of gay men and lesbians. It was easy for her to see things through my eyes, and vice versa.

When I wrote articles, I would send them to her, and she would respond with a thicket of insights that I had not thought of. Sometimes, if I was in California or she was in Texas visiting her parents, we would linger in the kitchen after others had drifted off somewhere, talking about ideas. Those conversations had a profound effect on me.

In 2008 and 2009, she told me about her work against Proposition 8 in California, which would bar same-sex marriage there. She was one of the people—perhaps even the most important—in shaping my own evolution on that issue well before I reconnected with Joy Tull, and her challenge required me to first confront my own personal bigotry against gay men and lesbians. Later, she counseled me, wisely, on the decision to write and speak about Baylor's policies regarding gay men and lesbians. I would not have done so but for her encouragement.

Katherine's advice was always astute, in areas large and small. When I was planning a conference at Baylor, I called her. When I was to give the commencement address at her alma mater, Vanguard High in Waco, I called her. She told me to talk about "love" a lot, and that is exactly what I did. When I was considering the move to St. Thomas, I sought her counsel again, and everything she said was right. By then, I had learned to do what she advised.

She had a trait that I see in the very best trial lawyers, the very best teachers, and the very best parents: she was a wonderful listener. She would lower her head a little bit, lean against a counter, and do nothing else but take in what you were saying. She was comfortable with being quiet as she listened, which is a rare and wonderful trait. If she wanted to clarify something or ask a question, her hand would come up, palm out, as a signal—the gentlest of signs.

Then she would nod. If she nodded hard, her hair would bounce, and sometimes she did nod hard. She understood, and she *did*—her intelligence could be sharp and fierce or soft-spoken, but it underlaid everything. She was, as we say in law, a "quick read," a talent that takes equal measures of intelligence, empathy, and critical thinking. It was those traits—intelligence, empathy, and critical thinking— that would frame her response. One did not go to Katherine Darmer if you wanted a simple yes or affirmation; she was too smart and honest for that.

One of my friends at Baylor, Francis Beckwith, called to tell me that Katherine had died. He didn't know how it happened exactly; that story came out later, and it was hard to hear. I didn't know that Katherine had suffered from depression, but she had. On that day, a Friday, she had left her home in Newport Beach and headed toward Chapman, which is in the town of Orange. She made a detour, though, and went into a six-story parking ramp near John Wayne Airport. She drove to the top floor and then jumped to her death, leaving behind two small children, a husband, hundreds of adoring students, and (more distantly) me.

Katherine's death shook me deeply, in part because I did not suspect, for even a minute, that she would take her life, but there was something more difficult, too, deeper and harder to grasp. Katherine was probably the person in the world who was most like me. Not only were our backgrounds and experiences similar, but we also shared similar personal missions and (sometimes) even our tone in advocacy. When I read her writing, it sounds like mine (or at least what I hope to sound like). She wrote with bold clarity and moral conviction. When she declared (at the start of one article) "Water- boarding is torture, and torture is illegal and wrong," I was thrilled by the passion and bluntness and truth of her prophetic voice.

So if someone so much like me could trip over that line from life to death so easily, where exactly was that line? How tenuous was my own grasp of what sustained me? Combined with Joy's assault on my vision, Katherine's death challenged my existence, my role on this earth. I left for Tennessee with a deep unsettledness.

Our trip to Tennessee was to be the first of two, both coordinated by Stacy Rector, the head of Tennesseans for Alternatives to the Death Penalty. Stacy was precisely the kind of collaborator we needed. An ordained Presbyterian minister and a native of Dyersburg, Tennessee, she was smart, welcoming, and well-connected. I had first met Stacy when she moderated my talk at the same Atlanta conference where I had met Jeanne.

She is (like all my favorite people) a little bit of a character. Jeanne had arranged these trips after running into Stacy at a Chicago gathering of death-penalty opponents the previous year. Stacy not only gave a riveting presentation about developments in her state, but later in the evening she made an after-dinner appearance in her other persona—as Tennessee's best female Elvis impersonator. As she sang on the stage, pompadour in place and medallions swinging, Renny Cushing danced the Twist with Sister Helen Prejean. It was a memorable scene.

Stacy had decided to make the most of our visit. This first trip would include no fewer than four appearances by me and Jeanne: a set of presentations at Belmont University in Nashville, a keynote address at a death-penalty conference at Middle Tennessee State University in Murfreesboro, a lecture at St. Henry's Catholic Church in Nashville, and finally a presentation of the trial of Jesus at Carson-Newman University in Jefferson City. The second trip would bring the whole crew down to Nashville to present the trial at St. Henry's.

On the flight from Minneapolis to Nashville, I fidgeted with words. Bob and Alice Baird had asked me to speak at a memorial service for Katherine, and I struggled to get it right. Setting that aside, I worked on my death-penalty lecture, a very different enterprise from the presentations in the trial. Nothing flowed, so I set it aside and slept, my dreams uneasy. Too much of what I was engaged in was death— those killed through capital punishment, the cruel deaths of Jeanne's sister and Bob's son and Renny's father, and the equally baffling death of Katherine Darmer. I had never had such a dark focus to my work in the past, and I felt the urge to escape it, to rent a car after landing, and to go off alone somewhere else, somewhere with less of this stench of death.

Instead, I was met by Stacy and Jeanne at the airport and packed off to a hotel on the fringe of Vanderbilt University's campus. Going from Minneapolis to Nashville in February is like being transferred to a magical land, free of snow and blessed with the warm breeze of spring. Even with that, I knew that my mood was different—quieter, more reflective. I don't have the rich understanding of death that Jeanne and her friends in the victim's movement do; senseless death was new to me. Fortunately, I had friends waiting for me.

Baylor is a small boat with a large wake. Despite my years of remove from the school, this book is full of people from the Baylor diaspora. That is not an accident; Baylor draws to it and often spins off people of a certain and memorable character. One of them was waiting for me in Nashville.

Even among the fascinating cast of teachers at Baylor in the 2000s, Todd Lake was striking. A graduate of Harvard, he went on to the Peace Corps and then earned a degree from Southern Seminary in Louisville, a Baptist centerpiece that was caught squarely in the middle of the battle for the Southern Baptist Convention between moderates (like Todd) and an ascendant conservative movement. Many of the moderates who ultimately lost that battle found a home at Baylor, and that history was an important subtext to understanding Baylor's role in recent Baptist history.

At Baylor, Todd had served as the dean of chapel, responsible for many religious programs at the school. He holds a similar (though broader) position at Belmont, where he is the vice president for spiritual development. While we were both in Waco, Todd was a friend and neighbor. We both worshiped at Seventh and James Baptist Church, too—the church that had hosted the first iteration of the trial.

Early on the morning of February 24, Todd and his wife, Joy, met up with Jeanne and me at a diner near campus. It was good to see my old friends, but they knew I was carrying a weight. Todd was thriving in his new environment, and he was eager to show us around campus, students calling out to him as we went by. Our talk was to be held in a large room in a campus center, and when we arrived everything was set up—a Belmont podium squarely in front of rows of classroom chairs stretching the length of the room. Soon those chairs were full, and I was watching Jeanne talk to the students about the death penalty.

It was my first time to see her speak to this kind of audience, and the reaction was remarkable. Many of the students were required to attend the lecture for a class—they had to be there. As one might expect, they were distracted as Jeanne began to tell her story. Some were tapping away on cell phones, while others had laptops open. A few, the most brazen, had headphones in their ears, listening to music.

As Jeanne spoke, that changed. As she talked about Nancy and her life, some laptops closed. When her gentle voice turned to the man lying in wait, gun in hand, texting was abandoned. By the time she got to the part of the story that affects me the most, where Nancy writes a heart and the letter "U" in her own blood on the rough basement floor, there was utter stillness, a complete focus. It was the most remarkable kind of storytelling I have ever seen, and undeniably riveting.

There was a moment, a tiny pause, after Jeanne finished the story of the death and before she turned to the death penalty where all in the room held the same question in their hearts: "How?" How can someone who has suffered such a loss show compassion? How could she even bear to tell this story? In that moment, Todd turned to look at his students and saw them stock-still in their seats, leaning forward, the phones and laptops and earbuds forgotten. It was the kind of spiritual moment that a college chaplain must live for.

When Jeanne was done, I was to speak next. I don't remember what I said, and it isn't very important. I was not the part of that morning that Belmont students would remember, nor should I have been. Jeanne's performance had been a tour de force and a wonderful example of what I try to teach about advocacy: that minds are changed not through argument but through narrative.

After we were done with the undergrads, Todd shepherded us over to Belmont's new law school. It was an inauspicious place—housed in an old maintenance building pending the completion of a grand and purpose-built new law building in the center of campus. Todd had arranged for us to address the whole community—students, faculty, and staff—in the largest room they had. Box lunches were handed out, and we were briefly introduced. Jeanne, sensing (correctly) that she had stolen the show with the undergrads, insisted that I go first.

We didn't really have a topic, so I talked about what a new law school would be like ten years down the road. I really was, in a way, a voice from the future, because in 2001 St. Thomas had been in exactly this same position. The news was good, though. St. Thomas had survived those early years and flourished, building a comfortable endowment and attracting good and motivated students to match the stellar faculty that had been cherry-picked from other schools. I could tell that they found this message heartening, and I loved the atmosphere of being in the middle of something brand-new and undefined. Rather than following traditions, these students would create them.

One of the new faculty members at Belmont was familiar to me. Alberto Gonzales had been the Attorney General of the United States under President George W. Bush and was the name on briefs in opposition to mine as I had sought to win greater discretion for judges in narcotics cases. It was a little startling to find him here in an old maintenance building on the fringe of campus. He hadn't been at our talk, but we caught up with him in his small office and ended up speaking with him for about an hour.

When we first sat down, there was a certain tension in the room. Gonzales had been a controversial figure; like my St. Thomas colleague Robert Delahunty and others, he played a role in authorizing and defending what the Bush administration called "enhanced interrogation" (which critics called torture) in the context of the wars in Iraq and Afghanistan. I suspected that many of his encounters with unknown people were unpleasant, based on the behavior of a group of protestors who often picketed my own law school because of the presence of Prof. Delahunty. I couldn't blame him for his wariness.

When Gonzales asked why we were in Tennessee, and we mentioned the death penalty, the tension only increased. Gonzales had been Bush's counsel when Bush was governor of Texas, and Gonzales was involved in the review of death-penalty cases there. "I'm guessing you are against it, then," he stated, with a bit of an edge in his voice.

We told the former Attorney General that yes, we were against the death penalty.

His response was one that we had heard before. "I'll bet that you wouldn't feel that way if it were your mother or sister or daughter who was killed," he said, challenging us.

I could feel myself lean forward without thinking as I prepared a response. My nemesis in the years-long battle over harsh crack sentences was now challenging me, directly, on the death penalty. Then I glanced over at Jeanne and realized that this was a question for her to answer. She nodded at me, understanding. What Jeanne did next is what Joy calls a "ninja move"—where one takes the energy of an opponent's blow and gently redirects it.

Jeanne started by nodding and telling Gonzales that she knows many people who have lost a mother or a sister or a daughter who feel exactly as he does—who support the death penalty. "But," she continued, looking sadly into his eyes, "that's not what I wish for my sister's killer." Immediately, Gonzales understood the line that he had crossed—he hadn't known that Jeanne had lost members of her family to murder. His mood now softened, and he offered deep condolences and apologized for the way that he had phrased his point.

Something changed right then; a switch was flipped. The three of us went from being antagonists to being acquaintances with a chance for friendship. Gonzales seemed genuinely interested in our project and acknowledged that the Catholic church supported our position. He revealed, with some bitterness, that he and Bush had often worried over execution decisions, despite the criticism of some (including Sister Helen Prejean) that the governor and his staff gave them little consideration.

He then told a story that I won't forget. It involved Carla Faye Tucker, a murderer executed in 1998 while Bush was governor and Gonzales served as his counsel. Tucker was the first woman to be executed in Texas since 1863, and her case received attention around the world. The night of her execution, the Web site for the Texas Department of Criminal Justice crashed because of the sheer number of people trying to find out what she ate for her last meal.

Carla Faye Tucker had committed a particularly gruesome double murder. She and a boyfriend broke into a friend's house to steal a motorcycle. In the course of the robbery, Tucker and the boyfriend killed the friend with a hammer and pickax. Later, Tucker killed a woman she found in the house, driving the pickax into her heart. She and the boyfriend were both convicted of capital murder and sentenced to death.

Tucker was on death row for fourteen years before her execution, and in that time she stopped using drugs, became a model prisoner (according to the warden), and was outspoken about her conversion to

Christianity. As the execution date closed in, supporters—including Pope John Paul II, Pat Robertson, Newt Gingrich, and others—urged Governor Bush and the Texas Board of Pardons and Paroles to commute her sentence to life in prison.

Fourteen years later, in a windowless office, Professor Gonzales was remembering that time. Governor Bush had pledged to commute death sentences only if a prisoner was innocent or if there was a problem with the process leading to conviction and execution, and neither of those factors were present in the Tucker case. Nor had the Board of Pardon and Paroles recommended clemency in the case. Nonetheless, Bush instructed Gonzales to go to death row and visit with Tucker. The death row for women was in Gatesville, not far from my own former home in Waco. It's a dusty town with a courthouse at its center and a prison on its periphery, ringed with razor wire.

Gonzales did go to Gatesville and met with Tucker. She was not a monster, so many years removed from her days as a drug-addicted ax murderer. They talked about the prison and about her faith. Gonzales then returned to Austin and met with the governor. When Gonzales sat down with Governor Bush, Bush wanted to know if Gonzales thought that the religious conversion was genuine. Gonzales told Bush, honestly, that he thought it was. Nonetheless, consistent with the principles he had consistently articulated about clemency from death row, Bush allowed her to be executed.

When Gonzales finished the story, there was that same sober stillness I had witnessed earlier in the day when Jeanne had told her story to the undergraduates. We sat in silence for a moment, and in that moment I felt a commonality with Gonzales. I knew, from my days as a prosecutor, that feeling of doing one's duty even if you were uncomfortable or uncertain about the outcome. It is a remarkable weight—in that moment the weight of life and death, nothing less. The fact that Gonzales remembered so much of that day, so many details of the experience, told me more than any conclusion he may have articulated. In the end, faith is what troubles us, and I saw that in him. He was troubled, as were we. As we left, he walked out with us, almost as if he did not want us to go, as if there were something more that he wanted to say. It was awkward, an unfinished ending. We all left with doubts, I suspect. Seeing doubts in Alberto Gonzales made him human and real. I liked him.

Jeanne and I walked out of the old maintenance building in silence. Stepping into the sunlight, we saw the new law-school facility being built on a nearby athletic field. We were both still processing the remarkable conversation we had just had, something that felt like planets running into one another, altering both of their courses. We started to walk across the campus, wreathed in quiet.

Losing an enemy is as jarring as losing a friend; each represents a sudden shift in the pile of Jenga blocks of our psyche. That displacement took me quickly to the tragedy closest to my heart. For a moment, walking in silence, I imagined falling from the top of that parking garage near the Orange County Airport and the utter helplessness Katherine Darmer must have felt in that second before death. That moment when death was certain—the moment Jesus experienced as he looked heavenward and said, " 'Forgive them; for they do not what they are doing' " (Luke 23:34), or the moment Karla Faye Tucker had been strapped to a gurney as people watched her die.

Jeanne knew better than to fill the silence, so we just walked. With a start, I remembered that we had another appointment that afternoon. Kent McKeever was a student at Vanderbilt Law School who previously had earned degrees at Princeton Theological Seminary and at Baylor. Through Baylor connections, he had reached out to me to discuss a vaguely defined project he was considering. I redirected our path to the quirky campus coffee shop where we were supposed to meet.

Sitting down at a rickety table, we spotted Kent quickly—he looked like a Baylor guy who had gone slightly hippie (which, at Baylor, can be achieved merely by growing a beard). He was sincere, forthright, and fascinating. His credentials could have opened the door to many high-paying jobs, the kind of work (and pay) that students dream of. But his hope was for something very different. He wanted to return to Waco and provide legal services to the poor. Specifically, he wanted to help people with problems related to housing, immigration, and employment. He was absolutely right in assessing the need—poor people almost always lose in civil court, are usually without representation, and have the deck stacked against them. Waco had plenty of poor people with precisely that need.

When Kent finished describing his vision, I leaned forward and looked up at him. I told him that he would make less money than he could working in a restaurant. I told him that the need was overwhelming. I told him that fund-raising would be a constant challenge. When I was done with my cautions, he gave me a confident smile. He knew all that and still he wanted to move to Waco and provide legal services to the poor. I had met very few people with such selflessness.

I was cautiously encouraging while Jeanne was gushing enthusiasm and admiration. It was typical of us—as an active public defender, she knows the exact places that the fabric of society has been torn and saw that Kent did, too. We told Kent about our meeting with Gonzales, but he seemed unimpressed with celebrity, raising his own stock in Jeanne's estimation. I offered to help him with contacts in Waco while Jeanne seemed ready to write him a check on the spot. By the time we left Kent to meet up with Stacy and her staff, it had already been a remarkable day. I was emotionally exhausted, and we were only a quarter of the way through our work.

The next day we drove down to Murfreesboro with Stacy. Middle Tennessee State is a quickly growing, fresh-faced school. That day, the campus was empty, cold, and windswept except for the building where our presentation was being held. Stacy had done a wonderful job setting up the conference, which targeted activist college students. Among those in attendance were two people who had been exonerated from death row. I had met others like them before, members of a remarkable fraternity of men who had been chosen for death despite their innocence. They were an important part of the death-penalty-abolition movement because their faces and stories made the cost of executing innocents painfully real.

When it was my turn to speak, though, there was an emptiness within me. Part of it was that feeling of falling like Katherine, of helplessness, that I could not chase away. Another part was more grounded. The audience before me was young and motivated, but they also agreed with me across the board. Like the audience for the trial in Boston, no one in the room was for the death penalty or even ambivalent about it. It ran against something I teach my students about advocacy—that to be a worthwhile advocate for change, you have to find an audience that doesn't already agree with you. I was failing that test of late. We weren't changing anyone's mind—not yet.

The next day, we spoke to a small group of organizers at St. Henry's who would help set up our trial to be held there three weeks later. It was our first encounter with a Catholic church, and we realized that we would have to adjust to the realities that the Catholic faith presented. While Catholic social teaching is squarely against capital punishment in the United States and other societies that can achieve incapacitation of dangerous criminals by other means, the people in the pews often disagreed. When this became clear in our initial discussions at St. Henry's, Jeanne whispered to a priest, "They're like a bunch of Protestants!" All of this, though, was just a prelude to our performance at Carson-Newman and our coming encounter with Randall O'Brien.

As we drove the three hours from Nashville to the hills of east Tennessee, I reflected on what it meant to bring the trial to Randall. First, it meant that we would finally have an audience I coveted, full of people who either supported the death penalty or weren't sure. Carson-Newman is a Southern Baptist school that draws a conservative student body. It's unlikely that they would be much like the progressive students we had just addressed at Middle Tennessee State. Second, it would bring Jeanne together with Randall, two kindred spirits who had already begun to influence each other. It was Randall, after all, who had prodded Jeanne to begin the process of reconciliation with her sister's killer, and it was Jeanne who had brought Randall a new and compelling narrative of tragedy and forgiveness.

Randall O'Brien is a remarkable man, by any measure. A Vietnam combat vet who served as part of the 101st Airborne Division, he returned to the United States at a troubled time. His native Mississippi was still in tumult as the forces of tradition tried to fight off racial equality. Randall's own hometown of McComb, Mississippi, was the site of the Student Non-Violent Coordinating Committee's first voter-registration drive in 1961, an effort that was met with violence and intimidation. Recovering from the war, Randall turned to faith and school. He ended up as an expert in theology at Baylor, where I sought him out to co-teach oral advocacy with me. For seven years, along with Hulitt Gloer, we learned from each other as our students got to watch. I learned on those afternoons how to give a sermon, something I now do two or three times a year. I missed Randall dearly when he left Baylor and was anxious to see him again.

We arrived at the Carson-Newman campus in mid-afternoon. It's a pretty place, set on a hillside at the edge of town. Someone (I suspect Randall) has put hammocks in every large tree, and on this spring day those hammocks were full of lolling students. After a few false trails, we found the president's office, and the three of us strode into the lobby. Quickly, the door at the other end burst open, and Randall ran out, face bursting with happiness, his arms outstretched. I got ready for the classic Randall hug, but he ran right past me without looking to the side. "Jeanne Bishop!" he said, sweeping her up in his arms until she was off the ground, feet dangling in the air. It was exactly what I had hoped for—the two of us knew each other already. For our entire visit, from the arrival through a concluding dinner hosted by Randall and his wife, Kay, there was remarkable spirit surrounding us, provided by Randall.

The lovefest between Jeanne and Randall was impressive, genuine, and extensive. Eventually, we introduced him to Stacy, and I resisted the urge to tell him immediately about her secret identity as an Elvis impersonator, something that I (correctly, as it turned out) suspected would be of great interest to him.

Time was short, so we were shown immediately to a set of adorable little guest houses. Jeanne's had a grand piano in it, and as I unpacked in my own little house, I could hear her playing hymns, her soprano voice filtering through the warm air. It was only a moment, though— we had to race over to the theater to meet up with our witnesses.

Outside the auditorium, our witnesses—Peter, the rich young ruler, the centurion, and Malchus, whose ear was cut off by Peter at Jesus' arrest—sat on benches waiting for us. My first impression was that they seemed young—but, of course, they were. They were also remarkably biblically literate, having no problem remembering the stories we would bring up in our examinations. It delighted them, really; unlike the people in other cities, these were men and women who grew up discussing the Bible every day. It was a joy to talk to them about who these people in the Bible really *were*—the earthy reality of their lives. I regretted that Joy and Sara weren't with us, as it would have been fascinating to watch them deal with these near-contemporaries.

The hour before the commencement of the trial was a flurry of activity, as we set the stage and Jeanne greeted some cousins from the area who had come up to see her. I furiously reviewed my notes, changing things on the margin with a red pen, until our judge arrived. We had recruited for this task yet another fascinating character: Stewart Harris, a constitutional law professor and host of the national radio show *Your Weekly Constitutional*. Professor Harris swept in with robes in hand and a student assistant in tow, ready for action. He proved to be an excellent judge and later included the trial as a part of his show.

We sat down at our tables as the crowd began to hush. Randall was there with Kay near the front, smiling broadly. I was nervous, in part because of Randall; he was one of my true heroes. Professor Harris began to make the introductions when Jeanne slipped over to my table and handed me a note. I unfolded it quickly since I was about to give my opening.

"Are we going to pray?" it read. I knew what she was referring to. Every time up to this point when we had performed the trial I had gathered all the participants into a circle for prayer before we began. With all the last minute rush, I had forgotten this step.

I looked over at Jeanne, annoyed. There was no way we could pray collectively now that the trial had started, and there was no point in her prodding me to do something that was plainly impossible. It felt a little bit like a distraction game that some trial lawyers play. I was not used to being angry at Jeanne or any of the others, but in that moment I was. When I stood to give my opening, the audience attentive, my unsettledness began to show. My opening was uneven and flat, as if I was thinking of something else, which I was. A lot of other things, actually: the meetings with Kent McKeever and Alberto Gonzales, that plaintive note slid over at the last minute, and that feeling of Katherine falling, of feeling that it was too late to do anything differently.

As the trial went on, my performance didn't improve, and neither did my mood. Examining the smart student playing Peter, I forgot some key evidence (the Gadarene pigs described in Matt. 8:28–34) and then improperly brought that evidence up during my closing. I stumbled once while stepping away from the table, and when I argued in closing, I was unconvincing. I don't always know it when things go well, but I am self-aware enough to know when they go poorly. It was a disappointing evening, and I couldn't bring myself to look at Randall.

After my rebuttal, the judge instructed the audience to divide into juries and deliberate. Usually during this time, I would talk to the others and eavesdrop on the deliberations, hoping to pick up tips for future performances. Not tonight, though—I did not want to be near anyone. I strode out of the auditorium and into the dusk, walking quickly across the quiet campus. Moving under the big trees, I was reminded of my dark-mood moments as a student back in Williamsburg, frustrated by similar subpar performances. If I stumbled in class or on a test, I would walk down into the restored village of Colonial Williamsburg and seek solace on the quiet, cobbled streets. This time, however, it wasn't just disappointment in myself. I was still upset with Jeanne, at the fact that she didn't consider that we had already begun when she slipped me the note and that there was nothing I could do to correct my oversight. In my mind, my poor showing was her fault, and I heaped blame on her.

By the main road, I sat on a bench away from the streetlights. A few athletes were still milling around, finishing runs, but it was quiet. I remembered another moment, not far from this one, where I also felt that sting of humiliation. In 2008, Bill Underwood (my Baylor colleague who was now the president of Mercer) and Jimmy Carter organized a massive event called the "New Baptist Covenant." Held in Atlanta, it was the first large-scale meeting between black and white Baptist groups in a hundred years. I had been on the planning committee and knew what a significant event it would be. In fact, I scheduled myself to be one of the speakers, albeit a minor one in a roster that would highlight Bill Clinton.

I had convinced my parents to come down to Atlanta for the conference. They were very fond of President Carter and hoped to at least catch a glimpse of him. Once they arrived, though, they were taken up by the whole thing—the preachers, both African American and white, were the best of the best.

When the time came for me to give my presentation, I stood before a good crowd in a generic meeting room deep within the Georgia World Congress Center. My parents were there, sitting in the middle of the room, and I was determined to make them proud. I began my lecture with a story and then moved quickly into argument against the harshness of the nation's narcotics laws. As I did so, I saw President Carter enter the room with a single Secret Service agent and watched him take a seat close to my parents. He listened closely to all that I had to say.

I imagined that when I was done, President Carter would stand up and talk about what a great lecture it was, and my parents would beam with pride. I was partly right; when I was done, President Carter did promptly rise to his feet to discuss my talk. He wasn't standing to praise me, however. Instead, he noted that such talk was insufficient, and he challenged me directly. "It's not enough to just talk!" he said, full of emotion. "You have to actually do something to make it different!"

I heard him to my very core. It was why I litigated the crack cases; it was why I went to Waco to press the LGBT question; and it's why I had started to do the trial again among those who supported the death penalty—because President Carter challenged me to do more. But now, standing in the dying light in the middle of Randall's campus, I felt like a failure. I had even failed to pray. For a moment, I understood how even for Katherine, someone so much like me, there might be a yearning for that feeling of falling. It was a thought that took my breath away.

I turned, and Jeanne Bishop was there. She had come out to find me, knowing something was wrong, and she had a few stray friends and relations in tow. Her green Escada suit suddenly looked out of place as she came over to the bench where I was. I shook my head as she approached, but she didn't stop. "I'm sorry. I was wrong to do that," she said. She looked like she was about to cry herself.

With that, I was back to myself, or something close to it. My hurt was small and petty, a thimbleful of water in the ocean compared to the grief of Katherine's parents. I didn't suffer what Katherine Darmer did—I didn't really know what depression was. I just missed her and was confused by the fact she was gone.

Behind Jeanne, a student was waving to us. The juries had returned their verdicts. We had to go in and describe the nature of death again to both our heroes and our students. Slowly, I got up from the bench and looked over the broad lawn and the hammocks at the fading last light of the day. I was not falling.

Outside the sanctuary in St. Henry Catholic Church, Nashville
(photo courtesy of Mark Osler; used by permission)

Chapter 6

Nashville

*T*hree weeks later we were back in Nashville, this time with Sara and Joy. The dynamic changed again with their reappearance, and it forced me to be less self-involved and more of the leader they expected. My first act on arrival was to survey the cars available at the airport rental lot. The company allowed you to choose from the cars available, and one stood out to this child of Detroit: a black Camaro that some clueless employee had negligently left available to me. I raced to it, jumped in, adjusted the mirrors, and peeled out of the lot to meet the others, who had already arrived.

While the last trip had been weighed down with deep meaning and interactions with people old and new, this trip started out with a much lighter feeling. As I got near to Nashville's downtown, I called to find where the others were and discovered that they were out shopping for boots. Reluctantly, I found them, but shoe shopping was not my first choice for an adventure in my new Camaro. Admittedly, I took the long way into town, missing the exit at least twice and enjoying it thoroughly as I accelerated on the ramp. When I arrived downtown, I found it full of people. It had a different vibe than my usual haunts, and I could see why musicians love the place. Music blared from bars with open doors, and crowds gathered at street corners.

In the basement of a boot store, I found the three women among a mound of boxes. Joy was schooling Sara on the difference between a real cowboy boot and "some Yankee shoe thing" while Jeanne kept an employee busy running back and forth with boxes. I decided to meet them outside once they were done and went to the street. At ground level, a gentle rain had started, a southern rain. It was familiar; for my four years of college in Virginia this same rain had fallen, steady and true. I watched the people go by and wondered what was ahead for us. It was our first time doing the trial in a Catholic church, and there were a lot of variables in play beyond our control. One of them, unexpectedly, was Stacy Rector.

When we arrived at the church the next day, Stacy was setting up in the back of the room, putting up a large banner over a table for the Tennessee Death Penalty Group. The table was covered in newsletters and pamphlets about the anti-death-penalty movement in Tennessee, the challenges they face, and what can be done to help and support them. We had never had anything so overtly opposing the death penalty at any of the other trials, and it stopped me in my tracks. I had been careful to avoid explicit advocacy during our presentations, and this was cutting against that ethic. I huddled with the others to discuss it, and the consensus was to allow it (albeit, over my objections). Part of that impulse was likely in deference to Stacy, who had done so much for us on both of our trips to Tennessee. In the end, the others were right; no one seemed put off by Stacy and her table.

Sara and Stacy hit it off right away. I shouldn't have been surprised; both of them fascinated me in a similar way. For one thing, both women had a background full of incongruous jobs. Stacy was an Elvis impersonator and a Presbyterian minister. Sara had spent her twenties in New York City, performing in off-off Broadway shows where everyone was barefoot, selling cheese with Mario Batali's wife, and catering private shopping parties for Goldman Sachs associates at Brooks Brothers, and had ended up managing the home healthcare and the redecorating of the apartment for Ralph Ellison's widow, Fanny, in Harlem. Now both women found themselves on the same side of an issue they cared deeply about.

We quickly prepped our witnesses, all of whom seemed well suited to the exercise. I found myself appreciating the maturity of these Catholic laypeople, who genuinely seemed to understand the project. As I prepared the parishioner playing Peter for his testimony, he leaned into me and whispered conspiratorially, "I'm a true believer." I wasn't sure if he meant that Peter was a true believer or that he was, but in a way it didn't matter. We had found that once a witness took the stand, the distinction between the actor and the role quickly blurred. In the Bible Belt, people were so used to putting themselves into Bible stories that actually doing it was effortless and natural. These were the witnesses that felt the role rather than learned it, a technique we had seen in Phil Steger at our very first staging.

As the crowd settled, I pulled our group and the witnesses into a hallway. This time I was not going to forget the prayer. Looking at the circle of friends and the older people who were tasked as witnesses, I breathed out and gave thanks. The energy was great as we walked in and took our places to the quiet buzz of the crowd.

Joy got up with no notes, walked to the middle of the dais where there was no podium, and gave a great opening. She seemed to have a new confidence. Sara had no choice but to do the same, and she did, decidedly leaving her careful notes on the table. The younger lawyers' assurance, however, did not spread to me. I was shaken by the last performance and my disappointment before Randall O'Brien and the others in Jefferson City, and that feeling hit me full force once it was time to go before the congregation. I consciously tried to recapture some of the fire I had shown in Chicago but failed. Could it be that I was bored with making the same arguments and examining the same witnesses? It felt that way when I was honest with myself. I was reusing my notes from the last time—something I would condemn if I saw my students doing it. Even as I finished my closing, I resolved to shake things up and make the presentation fresh.

This trip, though, was not about me. When the four of us were together, my most important task was to get everyone in the right place and doing the right thing, and I had accomplished that. Their talents, and those of the witnesses, were enough to carry the trial. As I wandered between tables in the social hall, eavesdropping on the deliberations of the jurors, I found that they were discussing Joy's and Sara's openings more than my closing. The students, at least on that day, had surpassed the teacher. It's a moment that is at once deflating and wonderful.

Sara was working on a research paper for me about the experience of the trial, and as part of her research she asked volunteers to come and speak with her after the verdicts were announced. As they finished deliberations, some did so—they came up in ones and twos to the table Sara had set up at the edge of the room. The first man she spoke to had his own idea about our intentions. "That wasn't about the death penalty," he said. "It was about comparing our laws today with the laws of Jesus' time." A glance at the Tennessee Death Penalty Group banner did nothing to dissuade him. It was a critique we heard occasionally—that what was most notable was the difference in law over the ages, particularly the criminalization of blasphemy. It was a disheartening comment, as that distinction was a distraction from our core point about the death penalty itself.

The next few people talked about how uncomfortable it was to be involved in the process. Finally, a woman and her daughter sat down. The daughter said she didn't even think about the death penalty. She focused on whether the prosecutor had proven all the elements. If so, she intended to sentence accordingly. What she didn't expect was that one of her fellow jurors would advocate vociferously for the sentence he thought was appropriate, death. It was obvious that the experience would stay with her. The idea that the death penalty could be imposed because one juror has a stronger personality than the others, even when Jesus was the defendant, had never occurred to her. This was closer to the impact we sought—she had discerned a weakness in the process Americans use to condemn some people to death and might therefore change the way she thought about the process.

When we were done at St. Henry's, we split up. We were to convene later for dinner, at a place with resonance for every one of us: the home of Matthew Cushing, one of the seven siblings of Renny Cushing, the head of Murder Victims' Families for Human Rights, and Matthew's late husband, Stephen McRedmond.

Renny, of course, had come to see the trial in Boston. From the previous encounter, I knew the story of his family tragedy—twin tragedies, really. Renny had lost his father in 1988 when an off-duty police officer gunned down Robert Cushing at the front door to his home in Hampton, New Hampshire, in front of his wife. Twenty-two years later, Renny lost his brother-in-law Stephen McRedmond in eerily similar circumstances: an active duty U.S. Army soldier, McRedmond's nephew Brendan, shot him to death in front of his home in Nashville, in front of his spouse, Matthew. We were now headed to dinner at that very house.

Matthew and Stephen had been a couple for thirty-five years but had been married only the year before Stephen's murder, at a ceremony in the state of New Hampshire, where same-sex marriage is legal. Renny, a New Hampshire state legislator, had performed the ceremony. It was marked by joy, particularly that of Matthew's elderly mom, Marie Cushing, who rejoiced to see the last one of her children walk down the aisle.

Not everyone was happy, though. Stephen McRedmond, a tall, bearded, larger-than-life man, came from a big, Irish Catholic, Tennessee family. That family shared ownership of some prime land close to downtown Nashville where many of them (including Stephen) had homes. Some family members disapproved of Stephen's sexual orientation and felt threatened by the possibility that another gay man, Matthew Cushing, might one day inherit Stephen's share of the property as his spouse. Another bone of contention was what to do with that property. Stephen was an ardent environmentalist and wanted to preserve the property's pristine creek and lush woods, where wildlife abounded. Other family members wanted to sell the land to developers to rake in profit.

Resentment exploded into violence when Stephen's nephew Brendan McRedmond, a twenty-four-year-old soldier stationed at Ft. Benning, came to Matthew and Stephen's home early on March 28, 2011. Gun in hand, he walked up to the front porch where Stephen stood. First, the nephew shot one of Stephen and Matthew's beloved dogs. Matthew was inside the house; Stephen shouted to him to run. Brendan pointed his handgun at Stephen and fired, killing him before turning the gun on himself to take his own life.

How to convey the enormity of this loss? Matthew and Stephen had been together, openly, for more than three decades—in the South. A whole community knew and loved them, from mailmen and grocers to leaders in business and the arts in Nashville. Stephen owned a successful manufacturing company in Nashville and a former meatpacking plant, the Neumhoff building, which he transformed into a center for the arts. Stephen and Matthew's unabashed love for each other was well-known; one of the stories told at Stephen's funeral, held under the shade of a spreading tree by the rushing waters of the creek by their home, was of how they would leave love notes for each other stuck on post-its throughout their house: on bathroom mirrors and kitchen cabinets. They built their home the way they built their life: with love, together. A wood structure at the top of a dirt road winding up a hill, the home the two men shared is full of meaning: books they collected, art given to them by friends, mementos of trips they had taken together.

When we knew we would be in Nashville, Jeanne reached out to Matthew to see if we could come by that home and bring some dinner; he graciously agreed. I volunteered to be the cook (Jeanne, who professes complete incompetence in a kitchen, brought the wine). I went to shop for simple, comfort food: good meat for burgers, potatoes, the makings of a salad, and pie. Jeanne and I arrived first and second; Sara, Joy, and Stacy were traveling together and, it turned out, had been delayed by an unsettling encounter on the way.

Matthew and Stephen's house is hard to find in daylight, much less in darkness. You pass through a gate and see several houses in the woods, all belonging to different McRedmonds. No road signs mark the way; in places, it's questionable if there is even a road. Pulling through the gate, it was hard to mistake the air of mystery that pervaded the place. Lost, Sara, Joy, and Stacy pulled up to a house to ask directions. Sara, social and gracious, got out to approach the door. Once she said Matthew's name, though, the woman Sara was speaking to backed away and just stared at her and refused to help. It appeared that the feud between the McRedmonds still simmered.

Meanwhile, I was already there. Matthew, a spare man with a gentle expression, welcomed me in. I sat down on a comfortable leather couch in the large living room, a fire flickering in a stone fireplace at one end. The tables were candlelit; colorful rugs were strewn around the floor. A single wooden beam ran down the center of the long, high ceiling—a symbol of the strong union of the couple who had built this house. Tired from the trial (it still exhausted me, even as it became familiar), I settled back on the couch when suddenly Stephen and Matthew's surviving dog, a big black Lab, jumped up by my side. He flopped his large head onto my lap and promptly went to sleep, snoring contentedly. I stroked his ears as I waited for the others. Was the dog on my lap lonely, I wondered, missing his murdered companion?

Soon came Sara, Joy, Stacy, and some of Matthew's friends, including one man who was a songwriter in this music town. I stayed in place as the dog continued his slumber on my lap. Hoping he would awaken, I realized it was tragedy that had driven everyone here—that is, everyone but me. I had sought out Jeanne first to do the trial because of her work on the death penalty, and that work was inspired by the tragedy of her sister's death. Next came Sara, who was looking for something to fill the spiritual void that had opened after her mother's recent death and all the tragedy that trailed behind it like cans tied to the rear bumper of a car. After that came Joy, who was driven into our project as she was driven out of her own family. And now we were here because of Jeanne's strong bond with her fellow survivors, like Renny and Matthew. There was no single tragedy but many, dissipating in the warm light of that room.

Eventually, I gently rolled the slumbering dog off my lap and headed for the kitchen, which looked out onto a meadow of grass and flowers. I gathered up the meat and stepped out the back door to start making hamburgers. Matthew had a nice grill set up near a picnic table in the meadow behind the house, with a view of the creek and a field full of oaks. It was dusk, and the fading light was filtered through the leaves of the trees. Stars started to appear, silver and bright in the darkening sky.

Taking in the moment, I lingered as I started the grill and shaped the burgers. I learned how to make them from an incarcerated uncle who taught me that there are only three necessary steps: to buy meat with enough fat in it, to use only salt and pepper to season the meat, and to turn the hamburgers only once. Faithful to his words (which were conveyed to me in the Metropolitan Detention Center outside Albuquerque), I carefully seasoned each side of the hamburgers and then set them on the now-hot grill.

I walked back inside, where the others were, and began to wash off the platter. Jeanne, Sara, and one of Matthew's friends were chatting nearby, leaning on a counter laden with bread and cheese and bottles of wine. "What are you doing?" Jeanne asked, her eyes widening. "Aren't you about to use that to bring the burgers back in?"

"Sure," I answered, "but I need to wash it off. It was just holding raw meat."

They looked at me blankly.

"The germs from the raw meat could contaminate the burgers if I put them back on there," I explained.

More incredulous looks.

Guilelessly, I announced, "I believe in food safety!" Somehow, this comment came off a bit too earnest sounding, and for months afterwards, to much merriment, I heard impersonations of myself chirping, "*I believe in food safety!*" Meanwhile, I wondered how Jeanne's and Sara's children (they have two each) had survived to near-adolescence.

When the food was finally ready, served on a clean platter, we took our places around the large table near the fireplace. The talk was gentle and calm, interspersed with laughter. Jeanne and Sara, both daughters of women who loved to sing and raised their children around a piano, began to sing, "Wouldn't It Be Loverly?" Eliza Doolittle's opening aria in the musical *My Fair Lady*. Matthew's songwriter friend went to his car and returned with a guitar; he sat down at the table and began to strum, singing in a voice quiet and low a song he had written. We sat listening, hushed and rapt, as the beauty of the music washed over us. The fragrance of the warm food surrounded us; the glow of the candles lit our faces. Wood logs snapped in the fireplace. The dog snoozed nearby. Outside, the stars shone down on the quiet woods and dark creek.

If our meal in Boston had been the Loud Dinner, then this was the Quiet Dinner, a communion of friends and strangers and songs. The ones who were missing because of the tragedies that led us there—Nancy Bishop Langert, Mary Sommervold, Stephen McRedmond—all would have loved that moment. It was their kind of party.

The Quiet Dinner changed us, perhaps more than the Loud Dinner had. It was there that we glimpsed the cloud of saints around us, who would love us in success and failure. They were there, infusing what we did and who we were each becoming. Then it was over. In the twilight, we drove out the long driveway. I gunned the Camaro between the spreading oaks, the river beside us and Oklahoma ahead.

Westminster Church, Oklahoma City
(photo courtesy of Mark Osler; used by permission)

Chapter 7

Oklahoma City

*J*ust one week after our performance at St. Henry's and the Quiet Dinner at Matthew Cushing's, we headed to a very different part of the country: Oklahoma City. At the heart of the reddest of red states, Oklahoma City offered us a striking concentration of death-penalty supporters. In going there, we confronted the feelings that endured long after the tragic bombing of the Alfred P. Murrah federal building by Timothy McVeigh in 1995. McVeigh was executed in 2001 after telling his lawyers to drop all appeals.

Not just the place but the timing of the trial in Oklahoma City was significant. The nation was in thrall to a compelling criminal law story—in Florida, a seventeen-year-old African American, Trayvon Martin, had gone to the store to buy Skittles. As he walked home through the gated community where he was visiting relatives, he got into an altercation with George Zimmerman, who was part of a local neighborhood watch group. Zimmerman shot and killed Martin, and the case became a flashpoint for racial tensions and an ongoing debate about the role of guns in American society. The iconography of the case was remarkable as well. Martin had been wearing a gray, hoodie sweatshirt when he was killed, and around the country protesters appeared wearing hoodies.

That was a new development, but some old news was haunting our trip. The performance of the trial in Oklahoma had been in jeopardy for months. Originally we had scheduled it at Crossings Community Church, the largest megachurch in the area with over five thousand members. The church was complicated—members' tithes supported both a free medical clinic (good) and a $900,000 house for minister

Marty Grubbs (troubling). Set amid a sea of parking lots and led by a charismatic leader, it is typical of the nondenominational churches that have grown quickly in the last forty years.

On a trip to Oklahoma City with a youth mission project, I had worshiped one Sunday morning at Crossings and found it fascinating and overwhelming. The music was great, a testament to Grubbs's background as a music minister, but the sermon seemed vague in its efforts to connect Scripture to real life (a problem I have with many sermons in many denominations). After the service, people crowded into the enormous coffee-hour area, which was in itself larger than any church I had been a part of. It was hard not to notice what an attractive congregation it was—going to church was a chance to look good, and they did. While it lacked the formal coat-and-tie monotony of High Church tradition, Crossings is part of a broader regional culture that favors physical attractiveness.

For months, we had worked with two of the associate ministers to set up the performance, which would fall during Lent. We sent them video recordings of a previous performance, which made clear that there was no express argument for or against the death penalty included in the presentation. Joshua Rofe, who was planning to film the trial at Crossings, put out a short promotional video, setting out his plans for the movie. The video was featured on Kickstarter, a fundraising Web site for innovative projects. Meanwhile, we researched Oklahoma law to make sure that our procedure would be accurate.

Then, just weeks before we were to present the trial, we began getting a series of anguished messages from the staff at Crossings. The problem, it seemed, was Josh's video preview of the movie. It had juxtaposed scenes of Timothy McVeigh with pictures of the church, and some on the church committees had taken offense at this, thinking it created a link between McVeigh and the church. They not only wanted the promotional video taken down, but they did not want the movie to be filmed in the church.

It seemed an odd concern—who would not be able to tell that the picture of McVeigh was to show the local context rather than something about the church?—but we quickly moved to assuage their concerns. Jeanne and I had a terse phone conversation and made our decision quickly. We would put a halt to the movie and get the video taken off the Internet. We were ambivalent about the movie anyway and realized that having the trial at Crossings was worth cutting that loose.

We contacted Josh and explained the situation, and he immediately took the fund-raising video off the Internet. Quickly, we reported back to the ministers at Crossings that we had solved the problem. Sadly, however, we were wrong. A few weeks later, we received a cryptic e-mail telling us that Crossings would not host the trial. The message alluded to dissent in the church over other issues and fear of the controversy that the trial could create while other issues festered.

We were shocked and angry. Nothing at all had changed about what we planned to present, and we had done significant work to set up the presentation at Crossings. On the phone with Jeanne, I could hear a note of despair in her voice. The presentation in Oklahoma City was personal for her because she grew up there. It was the mother of a close friend who had set up the connection to Crossings initially, and Jeanne had told her friends about our production.

Childhood homes are powerful forces. Jeanne had lived in Oklahoma City from fifth grade through high school. Her neighborhood in Nichols Hills, an enclave within Oklahoma City, was the setting for an idyllic childhood of family adventures, lifeguarding at a public pool, and Wednesdays and Sundays at church. At the Casady School, she was the female lead in *Carousel* and part of a small but remarkable cohort of students that included Clay Bennett (who later brought the Oklahoma City Thunder to town as Oklahoma's first major sports team) and her friend Megan Mullaly, who went from high school at Casady to college at Northwestern with Jeanne before becoming the actress best known for her role as Karen on *Will and Grace*. Jeanne's roots are deep in Oklahoma, and in her voice I could hear those roots being strained.

I am used to rejection, but that doesn't mean I accept it where it is unearned (though often my rejections have been well earned). Like the moment the previous year when I found that my piece on gay men and lesbians at Baylor had been spiked in the *Waco Tribune-Herald*, I determined that I just had to find another avenue for the same message. I told Jeanne that we would find a way to make it happen.

In the end, it was Jeanne who created that new avenue. Her aunt and uncle were members of a large Presbyterian church in Oklahoma City. She called and asked them to intervene on our behalf and convince Westminster Presbyterian Church to host the trial. Immediately, her aunt signed on for the project and implored her minister to bring the trial to Oklahoma. That is how we came into contact with Dr. Randle Spindle, the preaching minister at Westminster and one of the more compelling and engaged clerics we met during the journey. As quickly as Crossings dropped the trial, Westminster picked it up.

Oddly, I never did fully understand the issue at Crossings, which would have been a great venue for the trial. The below-the-surface tensions at the church don't appear to have ever come to public view. However, there is something distinctly and depressingly contemporary about Crossings. It is, in some ways, the religious equivalent of Facebook. On Facebook, everyone portrays the best parts of their lives; the struggles and failures are usually omitted. To look at someone's Facebook wall is to see a version of that person's life scrubbed clean. Crossings seems to present a Facebook version of Christianity: There is little or no controversy (at least visible to the public or the congregation), and the positive is always emphasized. This affirmative message is popular, as evidenced by the phenomenal growth of that church.

I'm not sure, however, that a Facebook church is particularly Christian. The faith Jesus described brought controversial things to the surface rather than bury them deep. Over and over, Christ immediately confronts people not with the Facebook version of their lives but with the real, whole one. When he speaks to the woman at the well, he is gracious and loving but does not hide the fact that she is living with someone who is not her husband. Within communities, he confronts the deepest and most controversial aspects without fear: the commercialism of the Temple, the demon among the Gadarenes, and the soulless legalisms of the teachers of the law. If Christ is *anything*, he is not afraid of controversy. Neither should we be afraid.

And so, with new determination, we brought the controversy to Oklahoma City. From our first discussions with Randle Spindle, we knew that he was someone who understood what we were doing. He wanted to know about staging—would Jesus be led in bound in chains? It was a startling question, and one with an obvious answer. Of course Jesus should be led in wearing chains. We just had not thought of it before.

There was an additional benefit to Westminster that we never expected—something that would give our message more reach than doing the trial at Crossings could have achieved. Westminster's service each Sunday was televised on an Oklahoma City station to over thirty-five thousand people. We would have an audience exponentially bigger than the number in the sanctuary—and far bigger than would have been in the seats at Crossings. Our disappointment had yielded unexpected surprises.

Sara had obligations back at school that would prevent her from working with us in Oklahoma City. Even though she was in my class, sometimes I forgot that she had the usual student things to do: studying for finals, writing papers for other professors, setting up the annual talent contest. She wasn't just *my* student, after all. Still, I knew that she wanted nothing more than to sit at counsel table next to Jeanne and stand to give the opening, Jesus behind her. To replace her, Jeanne recruited John Kenney, a partner at the high-powered Oklahoma City law firm of McAfee and Taft, who showed up well prepared and who turned out to be an excellent advocate. Joy, however, was set to come up from Dallas. She was still working for her firm, making money but feeling unfulfilled. She was bringing friends along to see the production and explore a new city.

Our first impression of Westminster was its size—it was by far the largest venue we had appeared in. While it was not a megachurch like Crossings, it was a large church with seating for eight hundred to a thousand in the sanctuary. As we came in, someone from the church mentioned that they were setting up an overflow room with a video feed, which seemed shockingly optimistic. The only publicity I had picked up on the trial at Westminster had been a small piece in the daily paper, simply announcing the event.

At Westminster, our greatest opportunity was also going to be our greatest challenge. The trial was serving as a Sunday service, meaning we would get the congregation that usually came at that time rather than people drawn to a death-penalty presentation. That was a wonderful break, because it meant that we would be freed from the self-selection that came with a stand-alone presentation—only people interested in the death penalty, one way or another, usually showed up. The corresponding challenge was that we had to ensure that our presentation took no longer than the one hour allowed for that service. There would be no time for deliberations by the congregation, and we needed to be careful in our use of time during the proceedings.

As we gathered in the sanctuary the day before our presentation, Rev. Spindle appeared with our witnesses. One turned out to have been a classmate of Jeanne's at Casady School, Tim Cheek, and they recognized each other immediately. Tim was to play Malchus, the slave who was cut by Peter during the arrest of Jesus. For Peter, an older member of the congregation had been selected because of his particular interest in the subject matter. Because so much of my evidence comes in through Peter, he is usually the witness I go to first in preparation and with whom I spend the most time. When Joy is filling the second chair, he is the only witness I need to prepare, since she handles the other one. Thus Peter had my complete and undivided attention. As usual, it was tricky because he is not really my guy at all—I am calling him as a hostile witness because of his close connection to the defendant. Thus, the best I can do is feel out what some of his answers might be.

As with a real trial, I prep witnesses in the actual witness chair if possible. This makes them more comfortable with the space and imposes a proper veneer of seriousness. After a few moments of conversation and simple pointers, I put Peter into the witness chair and started asking a few of the simpler questions.

"Do you know the defendant, Jesus?" I ask him, pointing to where Jesus would be standing.

"I've seen him," the man answered.

"And do you remember how you first met him?"

"No."

I knew that I was furrowing my brow with frustration. I had been clear that the person playing Peter had to have a comprehensive understanding of the Gospel stories. "So . . . do you remember fishing with your brother Andrew and seeing the defendant then?"

"I don't remember." Peter shot me an obstinate scowl. As I stepped away a moment to think, he called out, "It's not my job to help you!"

Quickly, I called Jeanne over. In a whisper, I started to describe what was going on. "Peter's fighting me on everything," I told her. "He won't say he remembers anything, even how he met Jesus."

Jeanne glanced up at the stage, where Peter was sitting with a growing scowl. "He doesn't know, or he just doesn't want to tell you?"

I hunched my shoulders to signal that I didn't know.

"I think we need to switch things up," I told her. "We don't have
time to fight through a difficult witness." She nodded her agreement,
gravely, knowing that for the first time we would be rejecting a prof-
fered witness.

Quickly, I pulled Rev. Spindle over and explained the situation.
He understood as quickly as Jeanne had, and I gathered the witnesses
to tell them there would be a switch: Tim Cheek, Jeanne's friend who
was scheduled to play Malchus, would now be Peter, and our current
Peter would take on the role of the slave. There were a few confused
looks, but it wasn't presented as a question but a fact. If we were to
finish in an hour, Peter couldn't be presented as an obstructionist.

In another circumstance, I think the original Peter would have presented a worthwhile challenge to me as an advocate. I was trained in
dogged cross-examination and spent years at Baylor training others
to employ the techniques for getting a witness to tell the truth. While
Phil Steger's eager and enthusiastic Peter was an epiphany to us,
there certainly would be more than one way to play the character.
The scowling parishioner was right in thinking that Peter might be
reluctant to testify against Jesus—after all, he denied knowing Jesus
three times when Caiaphas's servant girl went out looking for more
witnesses and encountered him. The older gentleman's portrayal
might well have been a true account of how Peter would have acted
if his denials had failed and he had been dragged into the chamber to
testify. However, we just did not have time within our allotted hour
to present that possible truth.

In finishing the witness prep, I looked over at Joy, who was laughing at my intensity. I knew that she was right; I was taking this one
very seriously, seriously enough to have rejected as a witness a vol-
unteer who had thought creatively about his role. The intensity she
saw was driven in part by the sting of rejection—since we had been
pushed away by Crossings, I wanted this alternate performance to be
perfect. Watching all of this, with the calm reserve befitting his job,
was federal judge Stephen P. Friot, a Bush appointee who was well
respected in his native Oklahoma. He would be overseeing our trial

and was a perfect choice: experienced, calm, and not a death-penalty opponent. It looked like we might need such a steady hand.

After our preparations were done, we retired to have dinner at the home of Jeanne's longtime friend Dixie Hendrix. Her house was draped along the shore of a lovely man-made lake. Near the house, a dock jutted out into the water, so Joy and her rambunctious Dallas friends jumped in every available boat and headed out onto the lake as I helped with dinner. It seemed wrong that Sara was not there, because it was her kind of scene. Though her replacement did an admirable job at the trial, he didn't balance out Joy the way Sara did. The two of them, I had come to realize, were a yin and yang that operated best in combination, their strengths and weaknesses filling the other's gaps. At a time like this, too, their personalities balanced—Sara would have been on shore with me, tut-tutting over the horseplay in the boats.

As dusk fell over what we learned to call Dixieland, a stillness came over me. I was being thankless to retain any bitterness about the rejection at Crossings. Through an unearned grace, I was here, in Oklahoma City, preparing for a larger audience and an engaged community. As the others played, I said a quiet prayer of thanks.

We arrived the next day to find that the church was already filling up. The ministers were on high alert, rushing from place to place in order to ensure that the sound was perfect, that the TV cameras were in place, and that the programs describing each participant were being distributed. We gathered in a robing room, but a flood of Jeanne's friends and relatives coursed through the doors. There were uncles, aunts, cousins, Jeanne's mother down from Chicago, the mother of an ex-brother-in-law, people from Casady and elsewhere, her doubles partner from a long-ago tennis tournament. Despite being gone for thirty-five years, it appeared that Jeanne Bishop was still pretty well known in Oklahoma. One of those to check in with Jeanne was Bud Welch, the man who years earlier had helped to change Cambridge fireman Bob Curley's mind about the death penalty. His own story was one rooted in Oklahoma City's worst tragedy.

Bud is a lifelong Oklahoman who grew up on a dairy farm not far from Oklahoma City and later bought and operated a Texaco station. He is a no-nonsense kind of guy, quiet unless there is a reason to speak. Every time I have been around him, it has been clear how much people respect him; even those who opposed him were gentle in their disagreement. Part of that gentleness was the product of Bud's overwhelming tragedy. His only child, Julie Marie, was killed by Timothy McVeigh. Julie was a Spanish translator for the Social Security Administration in Oklahoma City's Murrah Federal Building and died as she went to the front of the office to help a client just as the building was destroyed by McVeigh.

Bud had given us a tour of the bombing site and told me the story of how Julie came to be there. As we walked through the chairs that sit silent sentinel in that place, we found hers. Like the others, it was just that, an empty chair, and the power of the symbolism in that monument struck me hard as I stood next to the father of that daughter. It was a chair that would go unfilled at Thanksgiving, that would not sit beside a crib or at the back of a room in a school gymnasium during a Christmas pageant. It was just . . . empty, like the chair for Nancy Bishop Langert, or Mary Sommervold, or the chair for Joy in her own parents' home.

There is only one tree on the grounds that survived the bombing, an American elm. We stood under that tree as Bud told us how Julie tried to park under it on hot days. As he told us that, he looked up at where the building had been as if it were still there, as if Julie would come out at the end of the day to find her car.

His own road after the bombing had been one of deep bitterness. He later told Stephanie Salter of the *San Francisco Examiner* that when he thought of McVeigh and the other conspirators in the wake of the killing, he wanted to "see them fry." Over time, though, he began to see the negative effects of that anger. He was smoking three packs of cigarettes a day and drinking too much. Through the intercession of a nun, he traveled to New York State to meet McVeigh's own father after McVeigh's sentencing but before his execution. A breakthrough came when he saw a childhood picture of Tim McVeigh on the wall, and he realized that they both were going to lose their children to killing. Bud is a remarkable advocate against the death penalty in large part because he empathizes deeply both with people who still seek vengeance (as he did) and with those who love the condemned. It takes a large heart to do both.

Jeanne gives a lot of hugs, and she gives a big one to Bud, who fits in easily with this crowd. Though I don't say it, I think to myself that Bud is further along the same path that Jeanne is traversing, leading to a point where forgiveness shifts from words to actions and empathy. It is truly the road less traveled, and I have noticed that the fellow travelers treasure the company of one another. I am not in their group, of course, and I step away to prepare for the trial. Though Jeanne has more at stake here (with her family and friends abounding), I am more anxious.

My anxiety has two sources. One is the size of the crowd, evidenced by the hundreds of people now flowing through the doors. This is, in the end, my production, and I am ultimately responsible for it. If it all falls apart, I am at fault. There are a lot of loose ends and complications here, including the witness switch, the use of the trial as a church service, and the presence of a crowd that is largely hostile to our underlying message. If we fail here, we will fail spectacularly, both in person and on television.

The second source of anxiety, of course, is the usual conflict between my task and my faith. I find a place to hide, slip headphones into my ears, and listen to my usual preperformance psych-up song, Eminem's "Lose Yourself." Sitting against a wall, I nod my head to the beat of the song:

> You better lose yourself in the music, the moment
> You own it, you better never let it go
> You only get one shot, do not miss your chance to blow
> This opportunity comes once in a lifetime yo
> . . . .
> The soul's escaping, through this hole that is gaping
> This world is mine for the taking.[1]

Joy somehow finds me rocking out in the closet. She shakes her head and clenches her eyes shut to reflect the fact that my pre-trial ritual is something she would rather not see. "Time to go, chief," she says, and I follow her through suddenly quiet hallways into the sanctuary, where we take our places at the front of the room.

The room is completely full, with people standing along a back wall. It turned out that they needed that overflow room. According

1. Eminem, "Lose Yourself," Marshall Mathers, Luis Resto, Jeff Bass, 8 Mile Soundtrack, Aftermath/Shady/Interscope, 2002.

to the ministers, they had the largest crowd for a service in the last twenty years. As we come in, I put on my trial face, confer with Joy, and soak up the buzz of electricity that comes with a full and anxious room. Then from the back of the church comes a loud announcement: the defendant has entered. All heads pivot to see. Jesus, wearing a robe and chains, is being lead slowly down the center aisle of the church. Randle Spindle, it turns out, has a remarkable knack for theatricality.

Jesus was played by the bearded and somber Father Charles Blizzard, chaplain of the Casady School. The casting is inspired, as Blizzard brings a gravity to the role we had not seen before. The witnesses look to him as they testify, and it is apparent with every word of my condemnation that there is a person, fully human, who will suffer a death if the jury so finds. Something about that realization takes the edge off my presentation, and I have none of the fire and ferocity that I found in Chicago. My arguments are logical and plain. Joy notices and seems to think that maybe my psych-up music was a failure. On rebuttal, after Jeanne's plea for mercy, I try to inject some righteous anger at the threat Jesus presents, with some success. As I finish, a voice from the back of the packed house cries, out "Execute him!" and no one laughs. It wasn't a joke but a reaction.

Then, suddenly, it is over. Because we don't have a minute past the hour to take questions or allow deliberations, the trial ends with an exhortation from Rev. Spindle that "each must decide." Spent, we tumble into the hallways of the church with the crowd that has come to see us. People come forward with questions and ideas, pressing in, but I am looking beyond them at the others streaming past. To a person, they look troubled, as if saddled with a new load. I'm not sure if that is good or bad. Later, at a reception at the lovely home of Jeanne's aunt and uncle, I unpack the morning with some who attended. Like the others, they are unsettled, but I realize that it is a good thing. The first step to changing someone's mind is to trouble it—and we seem to have done just that in Oklahoma City. A year later, Jeanne would return for a reunion at the Casady School, and a flood of people found her to discuss the trial. It was still on their minds, some of which had, in fact, changed as they worked through the issues we had presented.

We had, it seemed, created something very different from a Facebook church moment. Perhaps not all of those in the audience were for capital punishment in the first place; broad brushes and assumptions based on appearance can often be wrong. As we left the church for the reception, some of those who approached us were clearly moved. One was Bud Welch, who seemed stricken. He recognized that this was a different kind of advocacy, and he said that more than anything the trial was a "great sermon." Jeanne and I both were still and humbled to hear this from him, someone who had already changed the world with a prophetic voice.

Bud was not the last person we spoke to, however. After the crowds had moved through the doors and we gathered our things from the robing room, an elderly woman approached Joy, Jeanne, and me. She clearly had been waiting for a quiet moment to talk to us. Moving slowly with a cane, she crossed to where we were and addressed us as a group. Looking severe, she said, "There's one thing that should have been different."

Jeanne, the kindest of us all, responded warmly, "Thank you! What should have been different?"

Pointing with the hand that was not holding the cane, the woman said vividly, "Jesus . . . he should have been wearing a hoodie!"

At St. Thomas in Minneapolis. From left: Susan Stabile, Jerry Organ,
Derek Hansen, Sara Sommervold, Jeanne Bishop, Mark Osler,
Joy Tull, Phil Steger, David Best, Hank Shea
(photo courtesy of Henry Bishop; used by permission)

Chapter 8

Minneapolis

*H*aving done the trial five times in the first three months of the year, we took a break for the next five months. I needed the time; there was a lot else going on. I had been chosen as the Richard Byrd Preaching Chair by St. Martin's-by-the-Lake Episcopal Church and delivered a sermon before that congregation and a few others. I also began to do more academic writing and devoted the summer to articles that later appeared in law reviews at Stanford and Harvard.

Then, too, I was due a little time off at "The Island." From age eight, I've been spending time in the summer at a family home on Lake Saganaga, which straddles Minnesota and Ontario; our place is just into the Canadian side of the lake. We share it with a similar Michigan/Minnesota family, the Frakeses. It is wilderness, and we are completely off the grid, cut off from roads, electricity, and running water. The newest cabin is one we built ourselves, with my dad and his friend Jack Frakes giving directions to a dozen members of both families. The time there is spent fishing, picking blueberries, swimming, and herding a combined tribe of children away from danger.

To get to the island, you need to know the way. The drive is the easy part: you head north on U.S. Highway 61, the same road Bob Dylan revisited and (far to the south, in Clarksdale, Mississippi) where Robert Johnson was said to have sold his soul to the devil. Then you turn left at the little town of Grand Marais, which lies nestled on the cold shore of Lake Superior, and travel sixty-four miles up the Gunflint Trail until it ends. From there, you get in small boats and pick your way through bays and inlets over cold blue water. It is useless to give directions; you have to see it.

The summer of 2012, I coordinated with my brother and sister so that we would all be there at the same time, allowing the young cousins of the next generation to see one another and run amok. It was a magical time. The youngest of the cousins, Will's son Stephen, led a remarkable musical performance on the dock. He was born for the stage and sang with all his heart as the sun faded behind the tall pines beyond the big water. The others followed his lead; it was hard not to as you watched the seven-year-old Sinatra lean into a song. It was a talent he practiced at home singing on the back step to an audience of one, my mother.

When I got back to school in mid-August, it was time to get my head back into the trial. My dean had asked that we perform it for the incoming students during orientation, and I had agreed. We already had three more performances lined up for the fall—one in Virginia and two in California, so it was a good chance to get back into shape.

More than that, though, I did it because the school asked me to do it. I realize how fortunate I am to have the job that I do; being a law professor is the best job you can have with a law degree in the eyes of many (including myself). Other jobs pay more money, but only as a professor could I have such intellectual freedom—not only in teaching but in the ability to choose a cause and pursue it through writing and advocacy in league with my students. I wanted to pursue this somewhat outlandish plan to try Jesus as a modern death-penalty defendant, and I did, with the love and encouragement of my employer. The least I could do was honor their request to do it for our own students a second time.

Though I often missed Waco, the move to Minnesota and the new law school at St. Thomas turned out to be a good one. I had tenure at Baylor, so I was able to start my new job at the same level and with an assurance of stability and academic freedom. As I left Baylor, a new president was coming in: Ken Starr, the former judge, solicitor general, and special prosecutor. I had met him years before when I moderated a panel he was on at Pepperdine. In fact, in the summer of 2010, as he was coming and I was going, *Wacoan* magazine asked me to interview Judge Starr. He sat down on my green couch amid my packing boxes for a few hours and talked about his new challenge. Starr is a complex character, with a skill set well-suited to the presidency of a school like Baylor. He is excellent at working a room and having one-on-one conversations, making each person feel like the only person in sight. He is also good at creating grand moments, like the vision of him running at the front of the Baylor line of freshman as they stream into the football stadium before a game. As Baylor requires, he talks comfortably about faith, and he is wicked smart. In all four of these ways, of course, he is like his former nemesis, Bill Clinton.

Clinton, of course, came up during the interview. "One of the things you did at Pepperdine was bring in very significant speakers, including Supreme Court justices," I noted to Starr. "Will you be able to do the same thing here at Baylor?"

"I hope so," he replied. "It's always great for students, but it's also great for the faculty, the administrators, and the staff to be able to see a renowned lawyer or justice of the Supreme Court."

"Would you ever consider having one of those people be Bill Clinton?" I asked.

"Of course!" Starr responded immediately. "I'd be honored to have President Clinton here."[1]

It hasn't happened, of course, but it could. If Jeanne Bishop can forgive the man who killed her sister and sit down with him over a bag of Doritos and a can of soda in Statesville Prison, I would hope that these two men of faith could sit and talk about the issues of our nation. It would be good for them and good for the world.

I had worthwhile reasons to leave Baylor, though, even with an intriguing leader like Starr taking over. In January of 2010, I was invited by my old friend Joel Nichols to give a faculty colloquium at St. Thomas—a short talk where I would discuss my work in progress. In preparation for that talk, I asked one of my students, Warren Wise, to prepare a portfolio for me with biographies of the St. Thomas faculty. It's my practice to do that when I have a small audience so that I can address people by name and know their backgrounds.

A few days later, Warren popped into my office overlooking the Brazos river with a binder in his hand, filled with side tabs. Before

1. Mark Osler, "Transformation: Q&A with Baylor President Ken Starr," *Wacoan Magazine* (August 2010): 33.

giving it to me, he sat down on my couch and said, "These people are really something."

As I dug into the materials he prepared, I found that he was right. The man who ran the clinics, Virgil Wiebe, was both a Rhodes Scholar and a Mennonite activist against the use of land mines and cluster bombs. The constitutional law professor, Tom Berg, was also a Rhodes Scholar, and like Joel Nichols he had a degree in theology as well as law. Of course, I also found Hank Shea, who was a legend at the Department of Justice as a groundbreaking white-collar crime prosecutor (on that page, I had written "HANK SHEA!!" as part of my notes). There was some eye-catching fact about each faculty member, and they all seemed deeply engaged in their fields not just as scholars but as people of faith who deeply desired change. They were my kind of people, even if I lacked the qualifications many of them carried.

Toward the back of Warren Wise's materials I found the intriguing description of Susan Stabile, holder of the Robert and Marion Short Distinguished Chair in Law. She was described as an expert in employee benefits and ERISA (the Employee Retirement Income Security Act), but that masked a much more fascinating side of Professor Stabile. After law school, she had gone to work at Cleary Gottlieb, a large New York law firm, eventually moving to their Hong Kong office. The move to the East was spiritual as well as literal. Having rejected the Catholicism of her childhood, she had embraced Buddhism. Eventually this led her to leave the law entirely as she spent two years in Buddhist monasteries in Tibet and Nepal.

She later came back, though, to the law and to Catholicism, though both were deeply influenced by her experiences during her twenty years as a Buddhist. Within the wide range of Catholic practices, she rests comfortably in a remarkable place, as an Ignation. Saint Ignatius Loyola was a Basque priest who founded the Jesuits, an order that has been remarkably influential, as evidenced by the number of schools that bear his name. Among other things, Ignatius emphasized the role of God in our lives at the present moment, rather than as a merely historical series of events, and believed, along with Blaise Pascal, that "the heart has its reasons, which the reason does not know."[2]

2. Blaise Pascal, *Thoughts*, trans. W. F. Trotter (New York: P. F Collier and Son, 1909), iv, 276.

Once I came to work at St. Thomas, the two-dimensional people described to me in Warren Wise's briefing book came to life. Virgil Wiebe, the crusading clinician, became my partner in developing a new clinic on federal commutations. Tom Berg, the constitutional expert, not only became a friend and advisor but turned out to be a skilled tenor—in fact, he had sung for years in the Fourth Presbyterian Church choir with Jeanne Bishop. Hank Shea has become a trusted collaborator on a number of projects, including the trial itself, where he has served as judge three times.

And then there was Susan Stabile. Not long after I dragged my old green couch into my new office in downtown Minneapolis, Susan popped in and rested her coffee cup on top of my cabinet. I'll never forget her first words: "Getting settled?" The significance of those words lies in their irony, because it is Susan who ensures that in matters of faith I never quite get too comfortable. On even the things I am most sure of, she unsettles my beliefs. For example, one of our early discussions revolved around creeds, which are recited in most Catholic and Protestant churches. One of the things I took away from my years as a Baptist was an aversion to creeds, resting on Jesus' directive that we " 'not swear at all, either by heaven, for it is the throne of God, or by the earth, for it is his footstool. . . . Let your word be "Yes, Yes" or "No, No"; anything more than this comes from the evil one' " (Matt. 5:34–37).

My aversion to creeds was reinforced through a chance encounter with James Dunn, the legendary Baptist theologian, at a Cracker Barrel restaurant in South Carolina. Dunn was often remembered for holding a Bible aloft and saying, "This is my creed!" Susan, though, challenged this idea. "Aren't communal prayers the same as a creed?" she asked, "or responsive readings?" Our debates extended long after her coffee cup was empty, and we eventually held a debate for our students on this issue. (Memorably, our colleague Reggie Whitt, a Dominican priest, said at our debate, "What I don't understand is how an Episcopalian can be non-creedal!" He had a point).

Now that I was settled into this remarkable place, I was ready to do the trial in a new way. Remembering the lethargy I had felt in Nashville, though, I decided to shake things up. We needed a new witness, and Jeanne had a brilliant idea: we could ditch Malchus the slave and instead use as a defense witness one of the most compelling figures in the Bible. John 8 tells her story. Jesus came to the Temple, and people gathered to hear him. The scribes and Pharisees brought before him a woman who had been caught in adultery and reminded Jesus that the law of Moses directed a particularly brutal form of the death penalty for such an offense—death by stoning. Jesus took his time to think, writing on the ground with his finger. Then he challenged them: " 'Let anyone among you who is without sin be the first to throw a stone at her' " (v. 7). Beginning with the elders, they drop their stones and go away, leaving Jesus alone with the woman.

The story itself was transgressive in many ways: it contradicts the Mosaic law; it turns power relationships upside down; and it ends with an unmarried man and woman alone together. The provenance of the passage is disputed, of course, with some authorities arguing that it was added to an existing text centuries after the events described. Still, it reveals once again a savior who overturns rules and upends authority, consistent with so many other parts of the Gospels.

More important, it shows Jesus directly confronting a live-wire social issue: the death penalty. Other than poverty, it stands alone in having received such a direct condemnation within the Gospels. The point is inescapable: Jesus recognizes the legality of the punishment but challenges the moral ability of flawed humans to impose such a final judgment. By bringing this story into our trial, we could add a new perspective to the discussions that would follow. We talked briefly about the right person to play this new character, the woman saved by Jesus from the death penalty. We were casting students in the other roles, and it would have been easy to bring in a young woman in a short skirt. It was, I think, Sara's idea to use instead Susan Stabile, a woman in her fifties. It was brilliant and perfect.

St. Thomas had the wonderful ability (and the funding) to build not only a faculty but a law-school building from scratch, and the result was spectacular. The school is centered around a four-story atrium, with fifty feet of glass opening onto the city. Above that atrium are balconies and open stairways, all directing the eye and spirit out into the world beyond those windows. In our first rendition of the trial, we had performed it in the ceremonial courtroom to the side of that atrium, but this time (due to the size of the audience), we were going to set up a stage in the atrium itself.

It wouldn't be our first time presenting in that grand space. A year before, Jeanne and I had a debate in that same place before the previous year's set of incoming students. The topic was the sentence of juvenile life without parole; she was in favor of retaining it, and I was in favor of uniformly allowing juvenile offenders a second-look review later in life through the process of parole. As the light streamed in, Jeanne told the hushed audience about her sister and the killer who took her life. Writing later in her book *Change of Heart*, Jeanne described that debate:

> We agreed on every important criminal-justice issue except this one. We debated each other as opponents on radio, on television, and in front of the entire incoming class at his law school one year. Osler spoke about children and mercy. I spoke about justice and fear. . . . I wanted to believe I was right. I told myself that the hundred or so inmates in my state who were serving juvenile life sentences richly deserved to leave prison only in a coffin.[3]

Now we were back in that same atrium. A screen was set up behind the stage, and we stood in a circle to pray before we began. It was Phil (back to renew his portrayal of Peter) who reached out first, and we held hands for the prayer. In that circle were Joy and Sara, who by now had become good friends and soon would become housemates after Joy relocated to Minnesota. Another student, Derek Hansen, was to play Jesus, and my colleague Jerry Organ reprised his role as the centurion whose servant was healed by Jesus. Hank Shea served as judge.

The final player was someone new, a talented St. Thomas student named David Best, who would serve as the rich young ruler. David had impressed me in my Criminal Law class in much the same way Sara had. He asked good questions, and his reactions to cases reflected something deeper than a sense of superficial legality. When he stopped into my office partway through the semester, I found that he had studied theology at Fuller Seminary under luminaries like Glen Stassen and had started a church before coming to law school. He was quick to tell me that the church he started had failed, and then

---

3. Jeanne Bishop, *Change of Heart: Justice, Mercy, and Making Peace with My Sister's Killer* (Louisville, KY: Westminster John Knox, 2015), 90–91.

he recounted the things he had learned from that searing experience. I knew from that moment I had an important new collaborator.

The assembled students hushed as Hank Shea approached the microphone and introduced the case. Like Susan Stabile, Hank represents a particular and important part of the Catholic laity who seek to comport their work with their faith. He speaks gently but with purpose and with the authority that comes from that rare combination of humility and strength. As he spoke, I looked past Joy to our opposing counsel. Jeanne and Sara were wearing nearly identical dark suits, and as they furtively conferred, their long, dark hair formed an opaque curtain. Joy rolled her eyes and whispered "poseurs."

The break was good for us, and there was a renewed energy. Joy gave our opening, did the direct examination of the rich young ruler, and cross-examined the centurion. I was to examine Peter and cross-examine the new character, the woman from John 8, before offering our closing argument. From the beginning, I sensed that the core of this one would be the new witness, and my hunch was correct. After Jeanne announced her as the next witness, Susan Stabile, wearing a long black skirt and a purple blouse, stood and walked tentatively to the witness stand. As she was sworn in, there was a trace of palpable fear in her. The fear wasn't Susan's—she was a tough-as-nails New York lawyer—but rather the woman she had become for this testimony. As she took her seat, she looked down at the ground rather than up at the proceeding.

Empathy is a core Ignation value, and it was clearly expressed from the moment that Jeanne Bishop had turned to Judge Shea and announced her next witness. One of Jeanne's gifts, born of years in the courtroom, is that she is a master of tone; she can signal a witness simply through the warmth in her voice or the lack of it. It is a subtle art, one that you have to watch for carefully, but I saw a master at work as Jeanne began questioning Susan. She started with a few kind questions on the witness's background and her living situation. Then she moved to the essence: "Ma'am, I know this might be hard for you to talk about, but have you been in trouble recently?"

Susan continued to look down. "Yes. I was to be killed by the authorities," she whispered.

Jeanne forged ahead. "What was it that you did?"

"I was lying with a man. He was not my husband." Susan's voice was one of a person trying to be strong. "They took me to be stoned."

"What happened then?" Jeanne asked.

It was at that moment, right then, that everything changed. Instead of describing the events in the Bible from the omniscient perspective of the Gospel writer, Susan told them as the scorned woman—from the literal perspective of a woman about to be killed who was thrown to the ground and had her face pressed to the dust. Stirring in her seat, she talked about being face down in the dirt and then turning to see someone.

"What happened then?" Jeanne asked.

Susan continued to stir, and we all were transfixed. "I heard the stones fall to the ground, one by one." She wasn't describing the men, because from her perspective on the dirt that is not what she would have seen. Rather, she described something that will never leave me: the sound of stones, one by one, falling into the dust harmlessly by the feet of the men who had come to kill her.

"Who did you see?" Jeanne asked.

It was then, for the first time, that Susan's head came up. "Him!" she exclaimed, voice full of awe, pointing at the defendant. There was a gasp and then a shocked silence in the audience. It was like light flooding a cave—Jesus was there among us. The student playing Jesus, Derek, froze in place as people followed Susan's eyes to him.

What was supposed to happen next was that I would rise and cross-examine the witness, poking holes in her story. Honestly, I can't remember if I did or not, and it really doesn't matter. We gave our closings as a blaze of sun came through the windows, and as we finished, I looked over at them all, David and Sara, Jeanne and Hank and Phil, the new students in front of us. There was a calm of revelation over it all.

There was a deep hope there for me. If my goal was to *see* Jesus, to have a sense of the very real person who walked the earth and told stories and taught wherever he could, I didn't quite achieve it that day, but I moved closer to that goal. Now I knew, through Susan Stabile, what it looked like to see someone look at that very real Jesus, a literal savior. Christ was reflected in her eyes. It was like seeing the light of the sun as it strikes the moon: a hope that the dawn will come.

Chapter 9

Virginia Beach

*T*he autumn of 2012 was a beehive of activity. My new clemency clinic was in its first full semester, and I was busy learning a whole new field of law. Clemency work is fascinating—it's all about the story of a person and expanding that story beyond the worst thing the individual ever did. Gritty stories, after all, had drawn me into law in the first place, back when I was serving papers to litigants in Detroit. My job was to deliver an envelope and get out of there as quickly as possible, but I found that hard to do. I always wanted to stay and see the place where a tragedy had happened: the surprisingly clean production floor of an auto factory or the horrifying main room of a low-rent day-care center. Even more, I wanted to learn the story behind each case; I often could be found sitting in my car, avidly reading the court filings before delivering them to the target of the litigation. I was particularly fascinated by the "facts" section of a complaint or brief, which publicly laid bare the complexity of human relationships in one-paragraph increments.

My first group of clemency students included Derek Hansen, who had played Jesus at the second Minneapolis trial—the nominal object of Susan Stabile's transformative expression. For the clinic project, he (and the other students) not only had to prepare a petition for a client, but I required them to spend two days in the prison getting to know the man whose story they would tell. Derek and his partner had to get themselves to the federal prison in Florence, Colorado, after they had first figured out how to get in to meet with the client—a process that often became a bureaucratic tangle. Other clinic students later included Sara Sommervold and David Best, and all of them had to struggle with the Bureau of Prison's confusing rules. That was part of what I wanted them to learn, after all: the reality of the maddening, shifting rules that consistently plague those who try to help defendants and convicts.

Right in the middle of that busy semester were several crucial events—we were going to be conducting the trial to three big groups of Christians who favored the death penalty. Two of those presentations, at Fuller Seminary and Azusa Pacific University, were close to each other in California, making them ideal for one madcap, West Coast tour. The third was perhaps the most intriguing of all our locations: Regent University in Virginia Beach, Virginia.

Regent is a fascinating and controversial place that has often been the focus of national attention. It holds out an ambitious vision for itself: "To be the most influential, Christian, transformational university in the world." That outsized goal matches the personality of its founder, televangelist Pat Robertson, who created a remarkable success on cable television but also sometimes veered to the warped extremes of the faith. He once blamed an earthquake in Haiti on "a pact with the devil" and suggested that "Gay Days" at Disneyworld might bring about earthquakes, tornadoes, and even meteor strikes. At the same time, he was clearly savvy and intelligent, and his opinions could surprise people. For example, on the issue we cared about, he had been surprisingly thoughtful although he remained a death-penalty supporter.

Notably, Robertson had personally appealed to Texas governor George W. Bush and asked him to spare the life of Karla Faye Tucker— the same woman Alberto Gonzales had visited in prison. Perhaps more significantly, in 2000 Robertson gave a speech at William and Mary titled "Religion's Role in the Administration of the Death Penalty." He began that speech by recounting a visit he had made to Florida's death row, and his favorable impression of two of the inmates there:

> I went in as strongly pro-capital punishment. Now, I'm going to pray with two men who are facing death in a week. Both of them have had religious conversions and are now my brothers in Christ. So what am I going to do with them? I could pray a prayer, "Oh God, give them grace to be launched into the next world," or I could say, "Oh God, please commute their sentences so that they won't face this terrible fate." I didn't know how to pray. They were in adjoining cells. I took the hand of one in this cell, took the hand of the other,

put their hands through the bars and I held both of their hands, and I said, "Oh God, I don't know what to ask for, but I ask for a miracle. Amen." I told them "God bless you and I'll see you later."

The next day, the Florida Supreme Court reversed both of their sentences of execution. They were released into the prison population, and the death sentences had effectively been commuted. The One, who in my opinion stands above all the courts in this world, had ruled that in their cases there would be no death penalty.[1]

Later in that speech, Robertson (in a strange twist of logic) argued that the executions of Christ and his apostle Stephen both argue in support of the institution of capital punishment. However, in answer to a question from the audience, Robertson seemed open to the idea of a moratorium and decried the celebrations that took place outside the prison when Tucker was killed by the state. In looking at Robertson's words on the issue, I find it hard to reach any conclusion other than this: like many people on this and other issues, his hard stance softened once he encountered the real people who would suffer the price of mercilessness.

The founder aside, one of Regent's more significant controversies also involved our new acquaintance Alberto Gonzales (whose predecessor, John Ashcroft, left to become a professor at Regent Law). While Gonzales was Attorney General, his senior counsel and liaison to the White House was a Regent Law graduate named Monica Goodling, who was one of over 150 Regent Law grads who found jobs in the second Bush administration. Goodling became famous for her entanglement in two Bush-era scandals. One involved the firing and replacement of seven U. S. Attorneys by Gonzales, a move that appeared to be politically motivated. A second centered on the politicization of hiring for career prosecutors, who are designated as Assistant United States Attorneys—my old job. During a hearing before the House Judiciary Committee, Goodling admitted that she "crossed the line" with hiring, and a 2008 DOJ report confirmed that she had violated federal law.

The connection to Pat Robertson, the Gonzales/Goodling scandal, and the subsequent election of Regent Law grad Bob McDonnell as

---

1. Pat Robertson, "Transcript of Speech on Religion's Role in the Administration of the Death Penalty," *William & Mary Bill of Rights Journal* 9, no. 1 (2000): 216, available at http:// scholarship.law.wm.edu/wmborj/vol9/iss1/12/.

Virginia governor (who was convicted of committing fraud while in office) gave the school a slightly sinister reputation, particularly in progressive circles. This seemed somewhat unfair to me. After all, my own alma mater, Yale Law, produced not only Pat Robertson but also such controversial characters as Gary Hart, Michael Mukasey (Gonzales's scorched-earth successor), both Clintons, and (according to one comic book) Batman.

My own, more positive view of Regent was influenced by an article in *The Atlantic* by Harvard theologian Harvey Cox that I stumbled across while doing a Wikipedia search in preparation for the trip. There, Cox identified himself as a "liberal protestant theologian" who had been invited to visit Regent and give a lecture there in the same courtroom where we were to present the trial. In the piece, he lays out his initial uneasiness about the place as a visitor from secular Cambridge, recalling, "As I sat reading over my notes and waiting to be introduced, a quartet equipped with a keyboard and an amplified guitar led the audience in singing lively gospel choruses. Some people clapped and swayed as they sang. I found it hard to imagine this happening in the mock courtroom of Harvard Law School."[2]

Cox found a lot that he didn't expect at Regent, including a thoughtful, balanced discussion, faculty with degrees from top schools, and an embrace of dialogue between liberal and conservative Christianity. In the end, he concluded. "Regent, it appears, is not so much a boot camp for rightist cadres as a microcosm of the theological and intellectual turbulence within what is often mistakenly seen as a monolithic 'religious right' in America." It sounded like exactly the place we needed to be. Regent, however, wasn't our first stop on our second tour of Virginia. Through Craig Anderson, we had met Michael Stone and Steve Northrup, who were leaders in Virginia's movement seeking alternatives to the death penalty. Through them, we had been asked to give a talk to congregants and youth at St. Mark's Catholic Church in Virginia Beach the night before the trial.

First, though, we met for dinner with Father Jim Griffin, the pastor of that church. He was a warm, engaging man who seemed to know everyone in the restaurant. From a naval family, he had been an

---

2. Harvey Cox, "The Warring Visions of the Religious Right," *The Atlantic* (November, 1995).

assistant to legendary Walter F. Sullivan, the bishop of Richmond's diocese and a leader of the Catholic peace movement. Sullivan had an active prison ministry, and Griffin followed suit. Working on America's second most active death row (after Texas, of course), Griffin personally counseled eleven men who had been killed by the state.

As we ate, Griffin described in excruciating detail precisely what that counseling entailed. He recalled one inmate who had asked him to recite the "Hail Mary" as the lethal injection was given. Father Griffin finished just as the killing agent did its work. As the man died, Griffin recited, "Pray for us sinners now and at the hour of our death." When he finished telling the story, there was quiet in the middle of the bustling restaurant. This kind of work creates those moments; it is not for those who fear quiet or deep and dark meaning.

From there, we drove over to St. Mark's and watched the sanctuary fill up, largely with teenagers. As we began, they were fidgety; it was clear this was something they were required to do for confirmation class rather than out of a sincere interest in the death penalty. At least at the start, that is. Once again, a familiar scenario played out: Jeanne Bishop, in a quiet voice, told the story of the worst moment in her life, when she was called out of the church choir to be told about her sister's murder. Suddenly, there was a stillness, as there had been at Belmont. These younger students, however, showed their emotions more openly. As Jeanne described the murder and what came after, mouths hung open. I looked over at Father Griffin as Jeanne spoke, and his eyes were not on her. Instead, he was looking at the faces of these children he knew, who were glimpsing a bit of what had made his own life something secretly extraordinary. When we were done, we walked out quietly, in the manner that some churches do on Maundy Thursday, into the humid stillness of a Tidewater night.

The next day I woke up early. Regent has a hotel, the Founder's Inn, at the center of campus. My comfortable room there had a good desk by the window overlooking tall pines. I spread out my papers and wondered how to present my case that day. The audience would be biblically literate, so I did not have to explain each fact in detail. But how could I convince these true believers that their savior (and mine) was dangerous?

It occurred to me in that moment that my argument could easily fit into a common evangelical theme: that Christ and modern Christians were threatening to a secular culture that included glorification of sex and a dismissal of the nation's faith heritage. It would be easy to appeal to that instinct and treat the lessons of Christ as threatening to contemporary social norms rather than to people like those in my audience and to argue that it would be the broader society who would kill Jesus, just as they were hostile to projects like Regent Law School. I rejected this idea, though. "Easy" is rarely good. A corollary to that Christians-versus-society mind-set was a tendency to see Christians as the victims of society—as misunderstood and oppressed people who in turn were happy to proclaim their victimhood. That rankled me, as Christians (and particularly white Christians like myself) were remarkably entitled within American society as politicians courted our votes and our sheer numbers dwarfed all other faiths.

Instead, I would make the argument that I had made in our other trials: that Jesus' message was a threat to our military actions, to our families, to our heritage, and to our capitalist economy. Each of these, of course, would be deeply challenging to the Christians present who viewed their faith as consistent with each of these things—and that is who I expected would be in our audience. After all, Regent sat close to the world's largest naval station (in Norfolk), wreathed itself in images of family and nation, and was largely funded by a remarkably successful business, Pat Robertson's Christian Broadcasting Network.

Outside, it was pouring rain. I recalled that in college, the Tidewater rain would go on for days, the water flowing seamlessly down the necks to the big rivers, the York and the James, and on to the sea. The imagery was powerful: each drop of water joining others to form a stream, and then a river, and then an ocean. It was humbling to know that I was just one drop in that larger sea of life. Here, though, an artificial lake had been built in the center of the university, and it stood between me and the law school. As I tromped across the campus, it became clear that the lake had seeped over its banks, and I had to wade, rolling up the legs of my suit pants before I entered the puddle.

Once in the building, I found Jeanne, and we explored the place while looking for the dean's office. Almost immediately, Jeanne noticed an anomaly. To the right of the front entrance was a table for the college Republicans. Almost instinctively, I looked to the left side, expecting to find a corresponding table for the college Democrats, but the space was empty but for a few drying umbrellas.

The dean at that time, Jeffrey Brauch, was an old friend and occasionally a confidant. He served as Regent's dean for fifteen years and had a wonderful skill set for the job. A graduate of the University of Chicago's law school and a valued teacher, he was also astute in explaining his school to often-skeptical members of the press. Obviously, we differed on a number of political issues, but at a deep level we had a lot in common, including Midwestern roots and a desire for an integration between our work and our faith.

Brauch is a striking, angular man who often wears a bow tie, and he was gracious as Jeanne and I tumbled into his office, still shaking off water. Almost immediately, Jeanne noticed a large portrait of Abraham Lincoln that dominated the suite. Brauch nodded and described his affinity for the Illinoisan, who looked both worried and optimistic in the painting. Soon we were discussing the trial itself, and Brauch explained that he had lined up students to help us as we had requested. Since we were performing the trial at a law school, we decided to have students there serve as our second chairs rather than bringing Sara and Joy along—a decision that met with disappointment and an electronic round of protests from Sara and Joy themselves.

A few minutes later, I was meeting with the student assigned to help me, an eager and intelligent young man named Andrew Cziok. I was surprised to find that he was from Minneapolis and then probed to find out the rest of his story. He was a remarkably motivated student, who spent one summer working for the U.S. Attorney (as I had in law school) and spent the other in India working on human trafficking cases for a Regent Law grad who had started an organization called the Freedom Firm. When a reporter asked him for his favorite Bible verse (the kind of question you get at Regent or Baylor but not so much at Yale), Cziok quoted Proverbs 31:8–9: "Speak up for those who cannot speak for themselves, for the rights of all who are destitute. Speak up and judge fairly; defend the rights of the poor and needy" (NIV).

Because he was not in a position to prepare at length, I gave Andrew only some of the duties I usually laid on Joy. He attacked them eagerly, though, as we forged into the courtroom and began preparing our witnesses. I eavesdropped and was impressed with the confidence he brought to the task. Preparing a witness is a difficult job because you have to let the witness know what is going to be asked, get a sense of what the answers will be, yet not tell the witness what to say (other than to tell the truth). To do it well requires two types of smarts: intelligence regarding the facts and law; and a different, distinct form of intelligence that lets a lawyer know and understand how a witness is feeling and will perform. Cziok clearly had both talents.

In a flash, the room had filled with students and faculty, and it was time to begin. Craig Anderson served as Jesus, and I could tell he was anxious to see how we would handle this audience. Correctly, he sensed that they were generally hostile to our larger point. Looking out at them as I would examine a jury during Jeanne's opening, I saw a variety of moods. Some were leaning forward, eager to hear her defense of Jesus, while others seemed aloof. I called Peter to the stand as our first witness and launched into the substance of our case—Christ's threat to the bedrock institutions of our society. Leaning in toward the student playing the role, I asked pointedly, "Jesus said that we are not to resist an evildoer, right?"

The student agreed, then tried to explain, but I cut him off, launching into my next point. Behind me our judge, a military man, looked over it all without betraying his thoughts. The audience was now engaged in full, wondering what would happen next. In my closing, I pressed my themes again, and Jeanne in kind went to the Gospels for her support, arguing that the jury should show mercy just as Jesus himself had shown us mercy.

As the juries deliberated, I did more surveillance than usual, trying to sit furtively in a spot where I could hear them talk. More than usual, their discussions ran deep into the biblical facts. One young man made a point that Pat Robertson had also mentioned in his speech at William and Mary: that Romans 13 begins with "Let every person be subject to the governing authorities" (v. 1) and then asserts, "Rulers are not a terror to good conduct, but to bad. Do you wish to have no fear of the authority? Then do what is good, and you will receive its approval; for it is God's servant for your good. But if you do what is wrong, you should be afraid, for the authority does not bear the sword in vain!" (vv. 3–4). I had to resist interjecting. I often hear this passage used to support the death penalty, but rarely has anyone made sense of it to my satisfaction—taken at face value, it conflates civil law with God's law, an exercise few people would accept in a world full of civil authorities that depressingly often have sanctioned genocide, torture, human trafficking, and racism. Moreover, the instruction to blindly follow secular law even when inspired by hate or retribution seems contradicted just a few lines later, as Paul writes, "Owe no one anything, except to love one another; for the one who loves another has fulfilled the law" (v. 8).

The juries reported their verdicts, and I lost again. No one seemed in a hurry to leave the room, though. A crowd surged to the front to speak to us in a rush that we had not seen before. If our goal was to draw them in, we had succeeded. Some approached to talk to our judge or congratulate their classmates who had performed, while others lined up to talk to Jeanne and find out more about her story. A reception was set up outside the courtroom, and I got myself some punch and caught up with Craig before heading out those front doors, alone. The students and faculty I talked to seemed interested but disquieted, and one man even seemed angry; if unsettling people was what we wanted (and it was), there had been some success.

Outside, the sun had come out. The campus was calm, with only a few students wandering back to cars. I walked back toward the lake, which was still swollen as the water that was meant to flow to a stream and to a river and then to the sea was instead held in place. I stopped and looked back at the law building, gilded with trees, as I hiked up my pant legs again and wondered if we were doing any good.

It often seemed to end this way, in calm and quiet, with me walking alone. Somehow that still surprised me. But it was my faith that told me that even when you do something good, the idea that there would be a parade for you was just a lie told in movies. It's more often true that when you do something to the good, you then find yourself in a puddle or worse.

As I passed one of the crosses on the campus—they all looked ironic to me now, as symbols of the death penalty—I considered what had happened to the man who hung on that cross, the man I had just finished castigating. His body of work was no secret. The Scriptures considered all that he had done, the teaching and the healing, the miracles and the wonders. The lawyers and leaders of the faith pondered it all, as did the political leaders. And then, knowing all of this, they carefully killed him in the most painful way that they could.

Sara Sommervold and Jeanne Bishop at dinner in Pasadena
(photo courtesy of Mark Osler; used by permission)

Chapter 10

California

*N*ext, we were off to California to do the third and fourth performances of the trial embedded in my fall semester. It was a grueling
schedule on top of my usual teaching, writing, and speaking, but it
had an unexpected and remarkable effect. When trial lawyers are
deep in a trial, it dominates their thoughts, and they are useless for
anything else. When I was in the middle of a criminal trial as a prosecutor in Detroit, I woke up at 5 a.m., my mind racing with details
about the case and the defendant.

This trial was no different, but the case was the Gospels, and the
defendant was Jesus. I woke up before dawn thinking about Jesus
and his teachings and went to sleep surrounded by the same cloud
of ideas. It was like the descriptions I had heard of the recently con-
verted, where they could think of nothing but Jesus. Somehow, I had
constructed my life in a way that my habits pushed me to do exactly
that. It was a remarkable time of spiritual growth, as I popped out of
bed very early and reached for the Bible to verify something remarkable I had seemed to remember. In the middle of the day, in a quiet
moment, I would reach for my weathered maroon Bible and add yet
another sticky note to a page in Matthew, noting something I hadn't
thought of using before. In a way, I was "on fire for Jesus," as some
people would say. I was learning all about him, though it did not yet
make sense as a whole; I still could not see him.

I would now be taking all those sticky notes to someplace very
new. Every audience was intimidating in its own way, whether it
was my own board of governors, the well-heeled parishioners of
Fourth Church, or the seminarians at EDS. Going to California

added a whole new factor, though. For Midwesterners, California can be a kind of fantasyland. It has everything our flat plains don't: the ocean, snow-capped mountains, deserts, and a culture that seems less focused on work than our own society of people with farm roots and farmer hearts. Even now, after dozens of trips there, when I fly to California I get a window seat. As the plane lands, I am pivoted to the outside, marveling at the palm trees, the curving frame of mountains, and the broad blue ocean beyond. I look out with longing at the Pacific, which is fundamentally different from Lake Michigan. Flying into O'Hare in Chicago, I know that on the other side of that water is Muskegon. Flying into LAX, the ocean you see ends at Tokyo and Fujian Province.

California is also exotic in that it is the strangest of death-penalty states. Generally perceived as a bastion of liberalism, it has steadfastly clung to the idea of capital punishment even in the face of multiple attempts to eradicate it. And, honestly, it is the idea of execution, rather than the reality, to which California clings. It has by far the largest death row in the nation (over seven hundred people at the time we visited) but only rarely executes anyone (thirteen people in the last four decades).

During the summer of 2012, I read that Californians would vote on a referendum that fall that proposed to get rid of the death penalty. The plate seemed set for us: we needed to do the trial in California during the run-up to that election. I quickly cataloged the opportunities we might create there. I was scheduled to speak at Stanford that coming February, but that trip would be too late, and Stanford (and Palo Alto) was too liberal to be a worthwhile target. We needed to go somewhere with a room full of people who either supported the death penalty or had not made up their minds. It infuriated me that much of the activity by activists prior to the election revolved around rallies at Unitarian churches or speeches at Berkley—places where everyone already was against the death penalty. It would make no difference.

As I pondered all of this, David Best wandered into my office. As he flopped his bag down on my couch, I suddenly remembered his connection to California. Excited, I cut right to the chase. "David," I asked, "do you think we could do the trial of Jesus at Fuller Seminary?"

In his calm, thoughtful way he paused for a moment, then said, "Yeah. That would be good." Then he walked out, called people he knew at the seminary, and it was done. As it turned out, he was able to arrange not only an event at the evangelical hotbed at Fuller (the world's largest multidenominational seminary) just a few weeks before the vote in California but a trial the next day at Azusa Pacific University, the second-largest evangelical college in the United States.

Because (for the first time) we would be timing our work to a specific political event, we decided to be more proactive about our use of the press. I had been writing every month for two and half years for the *Huffington Post* and used that platform to promote our push into California. The piece I wrote, "Prosecuting Jesus in Pasadena," began with a general description of the trial and ended with this statement summing up our purpose: "A society is defined, in part, by who it chooses to kill. If our society is influenced by faith, that faith should enter into those choices, as well."[1]

The *Huffington Post* article was a flop—while some of my pieces there have gotten as many as eight thousand mentions on Facebook, this one got fewer than sixty. Luckily, Jeanne knew someone much more influential than I was and gave him a call.

Maurice Possley won the Pulitzer Prize for investigative reporting in 2008 while writing for the *Chicago Tribune* after a lengthy stint at the *Chicago Sun-Times*. He wrote three books in addition to his work for newspapers. One of them was about a notorious Chicago-area mass murder, *The Brown's Chicken Massacre* (Berkeley 2003). On January 8, 1993, two men entered a Brown's Chicken restaurant in Palatine, Illinois, to rob the place. They forced the seven people working in the restaurant that day—two owners and five employees—into a freezer and shot all but one to death. One female, forty-nine-year-old Lynn Ehlenfeldt, had her throat slit. The victims, five men and two women, ranged in age between sixteen and fifty years old.

The community reeled from the merciless nature of the crime. For nine long years, it went unsolved. Finally, a girlfriend of one of the codefendants, James Degorski, turned the killers in. Degorski's accomplice, Juan Luna, gave a videotaped statement confessing to the gruesome acts they had committed the day of the robbery. The sentence they both faced was death. Juan Luna went to trial first, in 2007, at the Criminal Courts Building at 26th and California on the

---

1. Mark Osler, "Prosecuting Jesus in Pasadena," *Huffington Post*, October 11, 2012.

West side of Chicago. Luna had two well-respected veteran defense lawyers, Stephen Richards and Clarence Burch, and a tough case to make that his life should be spared. The prevailing sentiment in Chicago was that if any case deserved the death penalty, it was this one.

After the trial commenced, the family of one of the youngest victims, sixteen-year-old Michael Castro, held a press conference on the courthouse steps to make an astonishing announcement: they were against the death penalty for Luna. One female family member looked into the assembled news cameras and spoke, as if to Luna, words to this effect: "You showed my loved one no mercy. But we will show you mercy, because that is who *he* was. It is what *he* stood for." In the end, that family's hope was realized: Luna escaped the death penalty but by the narrowest of margins. Eleven of the twelve jurors voted to execute him; a lone female juror held out for the sentence he ultimately received: life in prison without the possibility of parole.

After decades of telling such stories and winning the Pulitzer, Possley relocated to California. Though he left Chicago, Chicago never left him alone. Like millions of others who had lived in and around Chicago (or so it seemed), Possley knew Jeanne well, and she reached out to him. As she knew he would be, Possley was interested in the project, understood what we were doing, and wanted to write about it. His piece for *Sojourners*,[2] an influential Christian media source, appeared just before we came to California. It gave me hope that we might make some small difference, building on the work of the dozens of other activists who had been working for months to create and promote the proposition.

Unlike Regent, the whole cast would be joining us in California: Joy, Sara, and David Best, who was to serve as my second chair as Joy shifted to the role of witness. She was troubled by that change, of course, but accepted my promise that there would be more trials where she would sit to my left. In addition, Jeanne and I were each going to connect with an old friend for meals and conversation. Hers was Jill Goldsmith, who had worked with her as a public defender in Chicago. Mine was Jeff Plansker, my best friend as a child who lived down the block on Harvard Road in Detroit. These were the

---

2. Maurice Possley, "Death Penalty for Jesus," *Sojourners*, October 15, 2012.

people who had taken a more-glamorous route to the coasts while we stayed in the middle of the country: the ones whose lives called out, "What if?"

Jill, who lived nearby in Santa Monica, had undergone a breathtaking metamorphosis from courtroom public defender in Chicago to Los Angeles–based television writer and producer for shows like *NYPD Blue*, *The Practice*, *Ally McBeal*, *Law & Order*, and *Boston Legal*. She had struck her own, unlikely path. After law school at Washington University, she had interned for U.S. Senator Paul Simon on the Senate Judiciary Committee before becoming a public defender. Jeanne remembered her as a beautiful brunette who always dressed impeccably—colorful, well-fitted suits and tasteful jewelry—and who relentlessly sought out opportunities to try cases. Jill didn't put in her time, waiting for things to come to her; she worked hard to move up.

After seven years in the Juvenile and Felony Trial Divisions, Jill stunned her coworkers by announcing that she was leaving for California to write scripts for television—specifically, shows about the law. She had an ample supply of stories, from her years at the public defender's office and good friends there with cases she could mine for story ideas in the future. She moved to Santa Monica with slender reserves and worked to get her new career off the ground. She studied the shows she wanted to write for and learned the characters: the way they spoke, the story lines, and so forth. It didn't work, though. Along with talent, drive, and good stories, it turns out that writers (like actors) also need a break.

Struggling to get a foot in the door, Jill went out one night, discouraged and needing . . . something. She opted for chocolate at a local shop but arrived to find a long line. She quipped to the customer next to her in the queue that she needed a treat; she'd had a really bad day. The stranger inquired why, and she told him. The stranger, it turned out, was a producer of one of the very television shows Jill hoped to write for. He offered to look at a script she had written, liked it, and wanted more. Jill was launched, and soon it was her stories that we began to watch.

Jeff's story was just as intriguing. We had known each other since our mothers had put us both in the same playpen as infants. Our fathers (along with Jack Frakes) were friends with one another from the advertising business—the original Mad Men, right down to the wreath of cigarette smoke and the snappy repartee. My dad worked with commercial photographers while Jeff's father was a well-known art director who worked on iconic campaigns like "The Heartbeat of America." They were both creative forces, committed dads, and fascinating people to watch work. I loved to go to my dad's studio and help paint sets or watch them construct a scene, nearly always with a gleaming prototype car at the center of the action (it was Detroit, after all). Their work seemed fun and glamorous, and unlike some dads they were usually eager to go to work in the morning.

While my family simply set out for the suburbs after we left Harvard Road, Jeff's family left the state—first for California, then to New York—before returning to Michigan while we were both in high school. I attended Grosse Pointe North while Jeff was a student at our arch-rival school, Grosse Pointe South. Inspired by the kind of work our fathers did, Jeff went on to Tufts and the Art Institute of Chicago for his studies.

There was one thing we had in common that ended up sending us in different directions: We both sought out a career in advertising, to do the kind of work our fathers made seem so worthwhile and interesting. Jeff, of course, pursued the art side. Meanwhile, when I returned to Detroit after getting my history degree at William and Mary, I tried to get a job as a copywriter at several advertising agencies in Detroit. That is where our paths diverged. I failed utterly in a series of initial interviews where I thought that I was being creative but probably was just being silly. Not everyone had the talent our fathers did. At the time, it was a crushing blow but one that led me to a minimum-wage job as a process server and then on to law school.

Meanwhile, Jeff was one of those who did have that talent, and he thrived once he was given the opportunity to make music videos and commercials. It is almost guaranteed that you have seen his work, which has appeared several years during the Super Bowl—what some view as the ultimate achievement in his line of work. Not only that, they are the good ads—the ones that are beautiful and moving and connect to something deeper than just the selling of a product.

Landing at LAX, I rented a car and navigated my way up to Pasadena. My first glimpse of our venue was heart stopping. Fuller Theological Seminary is an oasis of shade and green set in the heart of the city of Pasadena. Just a few blocks' walk from the heavily trafficked downtown, at Fuller the noisy air quieted. Pasadena's sunbaked sidewalks turned magically gray and cool, dappled in shade from trees overhead. Birds chirped merrily from the trees, their notes wreathing the small campus in gentle song. On the left stood beautiful old buildings out of which professors and students emerged, toting books and backpacks, chatting amiably. On the right, just outside a large refectory, picnic tables sat under the spreading trees, where you could bring a tray of food and sit, eat, and talk. Down a sloping hill, on the left, lay a quiet gem called the Prayer Garden, a place to sit and read or meditate, or to lie back against the soft earth and snooze.

I took a moment to walk the grounds and eavesdropped on conversations. The students could be found in pairs or small groups, talking intently about their classes and group projects. I had a reason to spy on them; they would be my jurors.

Once everyone found their way to Fuller, we sat down with our hosts at a rough-hewn picnic table set beneath a broad shade tree in the courtyard. I was immediately captivated by one of the professors helping to set up the project, a Baptist theologian named Glen Stassen. He had an easy manner, a deep intelligence, and the hint of a Minnesota accent. He eventually explained the accent. He grew up in St. Paul; his father was Minnesota governor Harold Stassen. He had built his own career, though, and is perhaps best remembered as the person who developed and promoted Just Peacemaking Theory. Stassen and his colleagues were immediately engaged in our ongoing discussion. Leaning over the table, he asked, "So, how does this matter?"

It was a good question. I hoped that it would seep into the larger dialogue over the death penalty and perhaps encourage Christians to have their faith inform their view on the issue. Jeanne and David agreed with me, and Sara was coming around to our view as the experience unfolded. Joy was skeptical, but she very much wanted to be a part of it. Sitting at the picnic with the theologians, Stassen's question made me feel like a bit of an imposter.

The next day we prepared our witnesses and practiced our arguments. In the afternoon, I met Jeff for lunch in Pasadena. He swung in front of the campus in a white Volkswagen Vanagon to find me standing under a tree with a gaggle of students. We were all looking up into the big oak, watching a drama play out on a broad limb of the tree. A large owl sat stoically, staring straight ahead, as two jet-black ravens tried to knock it off of the perch. One raven, then the other, would dive-bomb the larger bird and then sit on the next branch up and peck at it. The owl seemed intent on not showing any notice; it both stood its ground and refused to respond in kind with a peck or swipe with its large wings. Eventually, the ravens gave up on their quest and flew off in silence. The crowd below put down their cameras and began to discuss the bizarre display. "What was that about?" one seminarian asked another.

"I don't know, but it will show up in a thousand sermons," the other replied. She didn't laugh, but I did.

Later that night, we settled into a large lounge area off the courtyard and began arranging it into a courtroom. "Where do you need this, boss?" Joy asked, holding one end of a table. I pointed to a spot near the far end of the room. We never had the same arrangement twice, and only a few times did we get to use an actual courtroom. I genuinely enjoyed this part of it: creating a courtroom out of a found space. As Joy and I moved furniture, Sara did one of the things she was skilled at: greeting the participants as they came in and explaining the process. That kind of social place setting is not something I am good at, and I watched tall, graceful Sara at work with a sense of admiration.

The witnesses, having been oriented by Sara, then divided up among the two teams. They were students, and when we began to prepare them to testify—as Peter, the woman from John 8, the centurion, and the rich young ruler whom Jesus instructs—the nature of this seminary becomes important. They knew the stories well, of course, but they also were intensely interested in how we would animate them. As I talked to the rich young ruler, for example, we didn't just discuss the encounter with Jesus, where Christ tells him that to get to heaven he must sell all that he has and give it to the poor. We also talked about what that ruler must have been like—that he did have some humility in him. For example, he sought Jesus out for advice, and the story begins with the man calling Jesus "Good teacher." Also, when the rich young ruler gets the difficult message that he must sell all that he has, he is sad rather than angry and belligerent. It's not how a Hollywood movie would portray the character; there he would be an arrogant blowhard. The Gospels, though, make him real and relatable. We can't dismiss him as someone who is not like us, which makes the underlying lesson even harder.

The room quickly filled up with people and the buzz of anticipation. Jeff and Jill both arrived, and having them there made me a little more nervous than usual. With a few minutes to go before we started, I walked out into the heart of the campus, a long green lawn lined with tall trees. I sat on a bench in the quiet stillness of a Pasadena dusk. The others came out but did not say anything; they understood what I was doing and sat with me in quiet as the sun slipped into the ocean and out of sight. It was easy to see why David, a gentle soul, fit in here.

And then it was time to go. We entered the room, and a din of chatter silenced. All eyes were on us as we walked to the front. I took a microphone in my hand and looked out at them, the famous theologians and the eager students. It was my room now, and I did what I always did: I waited a moment before speaking. It might seem pretentious, that I am trying to build anticipation, but the truth is that I am just an introvert who finds public speaking a challenge. In that moment of silence, I am making sure that my first line is perfect—I say it once in my head before I say it out loud. But then I do, and we are off.

As the students leaned close to hear, something new came out of the direct examination of the rich young man. The ruler seemed chastened by the encounter with Jesus, genuinely sad, because he had to choose between his wealth and eternal life—he could not have both. The witness played it as a sympathetic character, standing in for all of us within a faith that describes riches as dangerous. It is a difficult message for modern Americans, including me. It is a condemnation of what (in part) we work for—a comfortable life for ourselves and our families.

As I wandered around the groups as they deliberated, I dawdled and eavesdropped. Some of the juries seemed tangled up on theological and historical points, such as the question of whether the trial itself was legal under Jewish or Roman law. Others, though, were straightforward in their approach, looking at the testimony on its face. "They're right," one man said in referring to our argument, "to say he wants to turn everything upside down." Among this group, there was some sympathy for that exact process; before they walked into the room, they had embraced the idea of Jesus as someone who sought to flip expectations and challenge the moral credibility we attach to wealth rather than poverty.

After the verdicts came in and Jesus was spared death yet again, we went to dinner with Jeff Plansker and Jill Goldsmith among our group. I was fascinated to hear their take on it, from the perspective of people who had left for a career in storytelling. Both found it powerful, and both noted the role of the most important players: the audience. It hadn't occurred to me, but by turning the audience into the jurors, we were drawing them into the story in a way that couldn't be done on television. The audience got to decide how the story ended—and they became the actors. We did not need to break down the fourth wall, because that wall fell as soon as the jurors stood, raised their hands, and were sworn in.

The next day, before I headed off with the others, I visited Jeff at his studio, which was chock-full of interesting bits of art and history. Tacked to one wall was a piece of our joint history: a poster that our fathers had made in the aftermath of the riots. It was an anti-gun piece, printed under the name Men United for Sane Thought (MUST), featuring a woman with a shotgun and urging people not to react to the violence by stockpiling weapons. There was that moment, back then, when our fathers tried to make something better, to play a role in healing. It was thrilling and sad all at once to know that they tried and also that they failed. The ruins only grew.

The next day we traveled east from Pasadena to the town of Azusa, which lies in the shadow of the San Gabriel Mountains. We Midwesterners climbed from our cars and gaped at the sight. Around us, the students at Azusa Pacific University were strolling to class, taking little notice of the tourists and their craned necks. It is a big, open campus in the California tradition, with large sun-soaked plazas and lawns marked with palms. It's no secular school like Cal–Berkeley or UC Santa Cruz, though; it is an evangelical university with ties to a number of denominations.

Our audience and witnesses were different here, with a majority of undergrads rather than the graduate seminarians we had met at Fuller. As we were ushered into a room to meet our witnesses, the age difference was striking; they seemed so young! Still, we found them to have the biblical knowledge you would expect at a school whose motto is "God First since 1899," and they were excited about the project. As we were parceling them out for preparation, I looked around the room at my friends. Jeanne was in a deep discussion with a member of the theology faculty; Joy was laughing with two of the students; and Sara was talking to David, who would be her witness to cross-examine in this iteration. Each of them seemed comfortable now with the process, unintimidated by the audience, and relaxed even in this unfamiliar place.

I didn't share their comfort, though. I felt the pressure of responsibility for it all and couldn't help but think about the piled-up work and rescheduled classes waiting for me back in Minnesota. I was in the role of being both tour manager and performer, which created a special challenge for an introvert: there was no chance to be alone while preparing to perform in public. Instead, I was running around answering questions, making sure things worked, and setting up a photo just outside the doors to the building, where a sign announced, "Tonight! The Graduate School of Theology Presents the Trial of Christ," before going on to explain the trial's relevance to the upcoming vote on the death penalty.

The hosts at Azusa had set up a platform for the trial in a hallway (the "Hall of Champions") and chairs down the length of it for a long, thin performance space. The arrangement initially struck me as odd, especially given that there was a theater adjacent to the hallway that did not seem to be in use. I could see the advantage, though, in that it would draw in people walking by—a tactic that seemed to work as the folding chairs began to fill up.

The judge appeared, and again we had a real judge to fill the role. Superior Court Judge Jon Takasugi is a respected jurist from a remarkable family. His father, Robert Takasugi, had been interned in the infamous Tule Lake Japanese internment camps as a child during World War II and then grew up to be a federal judge at the calm center of a number of significant controversies. It was in the elder Judge Takasugi's courtroom that automaker John DeLorean was tried for cocaine trafficking and in which Larry Flynt appeared wearing a diaper made of the American flag.

It turned out to be a particularly bad day for me. When the judge was introduced, the crowd began to cheer and whoop. This, of course, was not the tone I was trying to set, and I responded with a meandering, too-long explanation of the project. Fortunately, Joy gave our opening and was particularly effective. She has a deep, east-Texas accent that seemed to give her added authority before this crowd of casual Californians. My examination of Peter, though, was halting and incomplete; something—perhaps the annoying feedback I was getting from a microphone—had knocked me off my game.

Jeanne was not similarly disabled. As soon as she stood to talk with Peter, she seized the momentum by asking why the crowds flocked to Jesus. His answer is preserved in a YouTube video: "If you were ever in his presence, if you were ever there at any of those events, it's like nothing you have ever experienced in life. The words that he spoke, they were *life*."[3]

After the trial was done and the verdicts returned (another round of life sentences), we were joined by Haydeh Takasugi, who is a veteran California death-penalty litigator. As we answered questions from the audience, she described one thing that she includes in her closing when she defends a death-penalty case, and her words have stayed with me. After what sometimes will be days of testimony, she tells the jurors, "The only question is whether my client will die at the hand of God or the hand of man."

It was Haydeh Takasugi's words I remembered on election day, 2012. Most people were closely following the presidential race between Barack Obama and Mitt Romney, two men who offered very different visions and seemed to deeply dislike each other. I was focused on another race, though: California's Proposition 34, which sought to ban the death penalty. Early in the morning on the day after the election, I was crushed to find that it had failed by a few percentage points.

Some analysts blamed the loss on the failure of Governor Jerry Brown to take a position on the proposition (after the election, he simply noted he had voted for it, which was his first substantial statement on the matter). To me, though, it felt like a personal failure. What more could we have done? Should we have tried to perform at a larger venue, like Rick Warren's Orange County megachurch?

Should we have developed more media attention? I realized that I was elevating my own importance to ridiculous levels by imagining I could have turned the tide of the election, but my emotions couldn't seem to recognize that. I lacked even the humility of the rich young ruler. It felt like being a quarterback and losing the Super Bowl on the last play of the game.

A few months later, Jeff Plansker did, in a way, win the Super Bowl. His ad for Fiat, a gorgeous, tiny film set on a beach, got well-deserved raves. Jill returned to her work, writing good shows that I would point out to my students as realistic. They, in the end, were doing a much better job of showing a reality than I was. The cost of our failure, I imagined, might eventually be the life of a man at the hands of the state, killed by poisons pumped into his strapped-down arm.

November is a cold month in Minnesota, and when it was clear that Proposition 34 would fail, I stepped outside. The air was bracing on my skin as I stood in the night and my bare feet felt the frozen pavement. Above were too many stars to count, and in my city were hundreds of thousands of people. I was just one.

Tom Brooke and Jeanne Bishop at
St. John's Episcopal Church in Boulder
(photo courtesy of Mark Osler; used by permission)

Chapter 11

Boulder, Colorado

*T*he day after the election, it turned out that I also had something
to be happy about. I had worked hard for several months to defeat
a proposed constitutional amendment in Minnesota that would have
specifically barred same-sex marriage in the state. I had written about
the issue and spoken at several churches, something that alienated
some of my more conservative colleagues. One even told me that I
was "in error" and urged me to "repent." I didn't and haven't.

That evening, a celebration was planned for outside the state Capitol building in nearby St. Paul. I was sorely tempted to go but in the
end stayed home. After all, many others had a lot more to do with
that success than I did. In general, too, I'm adverse to that kind of
event and uncomfortable with victory laps. Before I left Baylor, the
students asked me to give a "last lecture." Tim Woods wrote about it
the next day in the *Waco Tribune-Herald*:

> At the end of Osler's talk, former student Dustin Benham, who
> recently worked on a case with Osler, asked what he would change
> about Baylor Law School. Osler said students should be more
> willing to lend each other a helping hand and give them someone
> to lean on.
>
> At that point, three Baylor theater students, planted in various
> places throughout the audience, stood and belted out Withers'
> classic song "Lean on Me." The audience soon joined in, singing
> and clapping along to the beat.
>
> With everyone focused on the singing trio, Osler slipped out of
> the room unnoticed and did not return.
>
> The moment was not lost on those in attendance.

"Everyone wanted a little bit of closure after finding out he was leaving," said law student Amanda Hobbs, who took two of Osler's classes. "I think that was his way of saying goodbye to all the people he's going to miss and are going to miss him."

Waco's 54th State District Court Judge Matt Johnson was at the lecture. He said his wife helped Osler set up the dramatic exit. "What he told my wife is he didn't want a situation where he was awarded any plaques or anything like that," Johnson said. "He just wanted to give his lecture and be able to leave, because I think it would have been difficult for him emotionally, otherwise."[1]

This felt the same, somehow, even though I was only a minor player in a large and long arc on the question of same-sex marriage. Instead of celebrating, I focused on a flurry of events over the following four months that were free of Christ prosecuting. In that period, I wrote op-eds for the *Dallas Morning News*, the *Minneapolis Star-Tribune*, CNN.com, the *Washington Times*, the *Huffington Post*, and *Sojourners*; spoke at Hamline, Tulsa, the University of Arizona, and Stanford law schools; and bore into a spring semester in which I was teaching three classes, including a big first-year lecture on criminal law.

In my writing and speaking, I was starting to move toward a more intense engagement with the issue of clemency. I found myself immersed in the details of the prisoners we were representing in my clinic. A part of me was jealous of my students, who were preparing to head off to the far-flung prisons to meet these men doing long terms for nonviolent crimes. There was an immediacy to it that I loved: this person was in prison, and we would argue for release of the captive.

This period of rest—at least from doing the trial—would come to a grinding halt at the end of March. I had three big events scheduled within the span of just ten days, in three far-flung states. I was to give a sermon in the historic Wren Chapel at William and Mary on March 17, 2013; prosecute Jesus in Boulder, Colorado, on March 26; and then take up the prosecution again in Austin, Texas on March 28. Of the three events, it was the first one that might have intimidated me the most. The Wren Chapel is at the heart of William and Mary's

1. Tim Woods, "Baylor Law Professor Bids Dramatic Farewell to School, Students," *Waco Tribune-Herald* (April 21, 2010), http://www.wacotrib.com/news/baylor-law-professor-bids -dramatic-farewell-to-school-students/article_c2f6e758-2246-5b47-9217-2e5f317f9de9.html.

oldest building, which was designed by Christopher Wren and built between 1695 and 1700. It is the oldest college building in the nation and one of the loveliest. It wasn't the room that was intimidating, though. The invitation to preach there came from one of the people I most admired, Professor Joanne Braxton. I had reconnected with her in the quirkiest of ways. She had happened across a blog post I had written that described two connected and fascinating events long ago, all of which began in her class.

One day as we were discussing a poem, one of my fellow students had a headache and was in obvious pain. Prof. Braxton paused and told us about something she had seen in Haiti, where she had done graduate research: the "snatching" of a pain like that. She explained that the snatcher would cover the forehead of the subject with his or her hand, rest and feel the warmth of that person, and then make a snatching motion. If done successfully, the subject was free of the headache—but the snatcher would now have it. It struck me, if nothing else, as a wonderful model of empathy in that it involved not "fixing" someone's pain or erasing it but literally taking it on as an act of self-sacrifice. Christ, of course, did this very literally.

Many years later, I found myself with a group of people on the roof deck of a bar near Wrigleyville. It was very late, and there was a small group of us around a table in the Chicago summer. We were talking about headaches, and I told the story of what I had heard in Prof. Braxton's class. One woman I did not know, who was about thirty-one or thirty-two, turned to me and claimed that she had a headache and dared me to snatch it. So I did. I put my hand flat on her forehead for a moment, feeling the warmth of her, resting her hair in my other hand, and then . . . snatch!

What happened next floored me. I didn't get a headache. Instead, what I got was a deep and profound sadness that was totally alien to me, like a dark cloud that filled me up. It was a specific sadness, too—the regret that I didn't have a child and might not ever have one. Certainly, this was not *my* cloud of dread (I was twenty-three or twenty-four at the time). It wasn't a guy thing—it was entirely hers. It was with me for weeks; I couldn't shake it.

It was my recounting of that story on my blog that brought Professor Braxton back to life for me; she wrote me a short note and wondered how I was doing. I wrote back enthusiastically, and we have since worked together on a number of projects. One of them was the sermon at William and Mary that week before the trip to Boulder. Since I had graduated, Professor Braxton had been ordained as a UCC minister and was not only a professor but one of the campus ministry group. Her invitation was the real deal.

Going back to Williamsburg always makes me eighteen years old all over again. Then, entering my freshman year, I arrived by plane at Patrick Henry Airport (my parents were on vacation, so they didn't drive me to college). I took a cab to the campus, walking up to my dorm with a stiff-sided Samsonite suitcase in one hand and a manual Royal typewriter in the other. The campus was a fog bank of mystery, humidity, and lush possibility on that August day. I still see it with those eyes.

As I spoke that Sunday morning, I was struck by the beauty of the light flooding into that ancient space. There are two large, round windows at the far end of the chapel, and the sun was streaming through. The rough wooden floor was illuminated with beauty; at one point during my sermon I couldn't help but to reach down and touch it with my fingertips.

The room was electric. People from different parts of my past appeared unexpectedly, the way that characters in Harry Potter books would "apparate" to a surprising location. Laurie Smith Dowdeswell, who had been my babysitter when I was in elementary school, sat opposite Tom Stanton from Waco. Craig Anderson and his wife, Lori, sat next to my son, Micah, who was with me to see the college. I took a moment to play out my first line to myself and then launched in.

It was a sermon about chaos, about the chaos of Lent. Think about it: Jesus enters the city triumphantly but then everything goes crazy. He tears up the Temple and is hunted down by the authorities; there is torture and death, and even his own followers battle the authorities as a slave is maimed. All this in just one week!

And then I talked about calm. I remembered how in college I would go at night to the empty Sunken Gardens at the middle of campus and watch the mist rise up and dance in the moonlight. It would hang there and envelope everything, wrapping up the students straggling home on the brick pathways. It was (to the nineteen-year-old me) a vision of the Holy Spirit, the comforter that Jesus promised us once the chaos was done. When I was finished, Professor Braxton took out a small pot of myrrh and showed us how to anoint one another in turn. I was last and turned to face my old teacher. Dipping my finger into the resin, I made a horizontal mark on the back of her strong hand. "Justice," I said. Then I made another, shorter mark across the first to form a cross. "Mercy," I murmured. She nodded, knowing.

The next day, I was to speak to Professor Braxton's advanced writing class. Prior to the beginning of the class, we met briefly in her office. She carefully pulled something out of a drawer and with the tips of her fingers pushed it to me as if it were a jewel. It was a book, a slim volume: Ernest J. Gaines's *A Lesson before Dying*. It was just that, only that, a paperback book, but that was everything; because to the people who know me, there is no gift quite like the *exactly* right book. And this was the exactly right book. Gaines's story revolves around a man condemned to die and the teacher who somewhat reluctantly reaches out to him on death row. I tucked it into my bag and wrapped it up with a t-shirt. I knew that it would hold deep meaning.

From there, the next stop was Colorado. Intriguingly, that trip would be a partnership with another of the people I knew from college. When people ask me who my best friend is, I don't hesitate in answering. It is Tom Brooke, who was a senior at the college when I was a freshman. We only had that year as students together, yet we forged a strong bond that has spanned four decades.

The secret to our friendship isn't similarity. We actually are quite different. Tom is a Republican, and I am a Democrat; he is a Southerner, and I am a Northerner; Tom loves pro sports, while I have only an occasional interest. While we are both lawyers, he practices in the buttoned-down corporate world of intellectual property while I have always been in the grittier trenches of criminal law. If there is a key trait to the friendship, it probably is this: we accept each other as we are.

In college, we were part of the same fraternity, which probably brings to mind drunk beer-guzzling idiots yelling homophobic comments. While that is the reality in too many places, our group was unusual, especially for that place and time. We were one of the few integrated fraternities on campus, and in fact our president was Michael Powell, the son of Secretary of State Colin Powell, who himself became chairman of the FCC. There was a moment in that fraternity house I will never forget. We were talking about potential pledges, and a name came up. One of the newer members said, "I think he might be gay." That newer member was then quietly informed about the half-dozen brothers who were gay and accepted as such. I learned more about tolerance in that fraternity than I had in my life up to that point.

Tom and I take a ski trip together every year to some Western state, and it made sense to combine that trip with the trial in Boulder. Tom would be my co-counsel, something that could never happen in real life because of our different practice areas. It was a wonderful thought—trying a case with your best friend, even if the defendant was Jesus and an adverse verdict was almost guaranteed.

The forum for the trial was St. John's Episcopal Church, a gorgeous venue on the edge of downtown. I had rented a little house nearby, which reminded me of the home Mork and Mindy shared on television in that same city. I was determined, however, to lay more groundwork in the media than we had in California, and we had some work to do before we got to the trial itself.

We decided to pursue two avenues. First, Jeanne and I coauthored an op-ed tied to the trial that ran in the *Boulder Daily Camera* on March 24. In that piece, we noted that without the support of Christians, there would be no death penalty in America. A study by the Pew Research Center for the People & the Press released in January, 2012, had reported that 77 percent of white evangelical Christians and 73 percent of white mainline Protestants supported the death penalty.[2] We offered up the trial at St. John's as a way for Christians to engage their faith with this hot-button issue, ending with this statement: "This state boasts a multitude of important Christian organizations and also a death row that consists only of African Americans. It is the perfect place for us to juxtapose faith and the death penalty, to bring to bear our deepest beliefs on one of the most momentous decisions we could ever make: whether we will take a life, permanently and irrevocably."

The second prong of our minicampaign was an appearance on Colorado public radio. The morning of the trial, Tom, Jeanne, and

---

2. Jeanne Bishop and Mark Osler, "Death and Christ," *Boulder Daily Camera,* March 24, 2013, http://www.dailycamera.com/ci_22851513/death-and-christ.

I gathered at the studios of KGNU-FM in an industrial park not far from the University of Colorado campus. For Tom and me, it was familiar territory, since we had met through the campus radio station in college and both served as the station manager for WCWM. We sat down on couches and were just getting ourselves some coffee when a producer popped out of a nearby office. "You are going to talk about the death penalty?" he asked. I told him that we were.

"You aren't *for* it, are you?" he asked, agitated. Apparently he had checked me out on the Internet and assumed that I was a Christian conservative who had somehow snuck past the sensors at public radio headquarters. The answer to that question was actually a little complicated. Jeanne and I, of course, were quite clearly against capital punishment, but Tom was not. I liked the idea of involving an agnostic on the issue in the trial; it brought to the surface the deep complexity of the issue. When we went on the air, in fact, we revealed our own difference of opinion. I liked that; there was an intellectual honesty in having someone aboard who was not in agreement with us.

When we got to the church later that day we met up with the rector, an energetic woman named Susan Springer. She and Jeanne bonded immediately, for they shared a common energy. Our witnesses, as usual drawn from the congregation, were ready to go. Susan had prepared them with the relevant passages, anticipating each role. In those few hours before the trial, though, amid the hurly-burly of preparation, we received some deflating news. As in California, our timing for this presentation was deliberate: the trial was due to take place on the day of a scheduled vote in the Colorado legislature on a bill to abolish the death penalty. Coloradans who opposed the death penalty were hopeful about the chances of passage, and so were we.

We had reason to be optimistic. Use of the death penalty had dwindled; no executions had taken place in Colorado since 1997. A Democratic governor, John Hickenlooper, held office. Only three people were on Colorado's death row; one of them, however, had murdered a relative of a member of the Colorado legislature, Democrat Rhonda Fields. Fields's son and his fiancé were gunned down just ahead of his scheduled testimony in a murder trial. The young man's killer, Sir Mario Owens, was sentenced to death, as was the man who ordered the hit, Robert Ray. Rhonda Fields strongly favored keeping death sentences, but was one of the few Democrats in the legislature to do so.

In the weeks leading up to our trial, Democrats, who controlled the Colorado House of Representatives, believed they had enough votes to pass an abolition bill out of committee and through both chambers of the Colorado legislature. One of the bill's cosponsors, Claire Levy, a Democrat from Boulder, said that she not only had the votes to pass the bill but that those votes were bipartisan. We thus hadn't counted on an unlikely voice raising doubts about getting rid of the death penalty: that of Governor Hickenlooper. Even as we were preparing for the trial, the governor was attending a luncheon with the House Democratic caucus in a building across the street from the Capitol. Just one hour before a House committee was scheduled to vote on the death penalty abolition bill, Hickenlooper surprised lawmakers at the luncheon by questioning whether Coloradans were ready for abolition. Some members of the legislature feared a veto and voted against the bill, six to four.

Tom, Jeanne, and I were gathered with our witnesses, prepping for the trial, when a church member came in with a grave face and stunning news: the abolition bill we had all hoped would pass had died in committee that very day. The legislature would not be able to vote again on the matter for about another year. The broader project had failed before we even got to raise our voices.

Jeanne's first chair was a member of the congregation, and as I looked across the stage at them, I could see a certain darkness in her mood. Sometimes I forgot that this was personal to her—that in her own life, ideas about death and punishment were not an abstraction or simple policy debate. She had been all over the world to decry the sentence many believed her sister's killer deserved, and her commitment was that deep belief of a contrarian who defies expectations and must dig in to survive. To her, the passing of this opportunity to add another state to the abolition states cut deep. It was linked in her to the loss of her beloved sister, who wrote "Love you" in her own blood as she died, literal blood of atonement shed for those that Jeanne now sought to save. She was the apostle carrying on the message conveyed in death.

For me, there was no such loss or deep connection, just a spiritual and philosophical belief that the death penalty was wrong. Of course, the old friend sitting next to me did not even have that; Tom was an unashamed Christian but agnostic on the death penalty. After I introduced the trial, I watched him square his papers, walk to the well of our makeshift court, and look purposefully at the audience. He had an air of authority to him, one born of success in courtrooms and boardrooms across the country. When he gave the opening, it rang differently than it did when Joy or I performed the same function; he had an objectivity that added to the power of the message. His relationship to the defendant was not as complex as the welter of conflicting emotions that Joy or I brought with us when we talked about Jesus.

There was something else different, too. As the sun faded in the evening, the church was dark in a way that many old, stone Episcopal churches are, including my home church of St. Stephen's back in Minnesota. Even when lit, the sanctuary remained in shadow. When I cried out that night for jurors to kill Jesus, my words hung in the air, heavy. Looking back at pictures of that event I see the usual groups of jurors huddled together, leaning in toward one another and eagerly discussing the case. My memory of it, though, is of that dearth of light and a sense of moving slowly in relation to my friend Tom, who was not so troubled by the political developments of that day.

When we were done, with the verdicts returned, I stepped through the big red doors of the church with Tom as Jeanne debriefed with the grateful and gracious rector. "I'll bet they have good record stores here," Tom said, looking off toward Boulder's bustling downtown. It was exactly the right thing to say. Friends can do that, in just a few words. In the cool evening air we set out in that postcard-perfect college town, in search of old vinyl records and songs about heartbreak.

Mary Darden, Bob Darden, Joy Tull, and Jeanne Bishop
before the trial in Austin

(photo courtesy of Mark Osler; used by permission)

Chapter 12

Austin

*H*eading back to the airport with Tom, I could tell that he was a little jealous that he couldn't go on with me to the next stop; in just two days I would be in Austin, Texas. Austin is a city that is at once both low-key and flashy. I read once that Minneapolis is white wine after the opera while St. Paul is a beer after mowing the lawn. The brilliance of Austin is that it is a beer while watching the opera.

I had two good reasons to be happy to be headed back to Texas. The first was that we needed to be there if we really wanted to be speaking where it mattered. It was a bit of an embarrassment to me that we were working on a death-penalty project but hadn't yet been to the state that executes more people than any other. From my experience some twelve years earlier in Waco, I knew how important it was to bring together Texans' belief in the death penalty with their belief in Christ and just how explosive that juxtaposition could be.

The second had to do with something deep within me. Texas Baptists are a particular strain within the larger national body, and my ten years among them in Waco had changed me. As with many things Texan, the Baptists there are fiercely independent. When a fundamentalist wave swept through the Southern Baptist Convention in the 1980s, that group sought to capture both the Baptist General Convention of Texas (BGCT) and Baylor University (which is affiliated with the BGCT). Both the BGCT and Baylor fended off the threatened control by fundamentalists, and sometimes you will hear "Texas Baptists" described as if they are a distinct denomination. In fact, they are a loose collective of Southern Baptists, more liberal

American Baptists, and some churches (such as my own beloved Seventh and James) that are simply affiliated with the BGCT.

Within Southern Baptists, there is a strong strain of "soul competence," which is closely related to the idea of "priesthood of the believer." Taken together, these two principles tell parishioners at a Texas Baptist church like Seventh and James that each individual must determine his or her core beliefs within the broad outlines of the Christian faith and that each soul is competent to discern truth from the Bible and from one's relationship with God. In other words, "church teaching" in these churches is much less important than individual conscience and self-determination. That is one reason that many Texas Baptists reject creeds—they cut against the idea that group belief is more important than individual belief.

Given the fierce independence of Texas Baptist churches and the unmistakable trait of individualism within those churches, theological discussions can be pretty wild and wooly, especially in those churches with a high level of education where everyone knows his or her Bible and most people seemed to see themselves as theological experts of some kind. We were headed straight into the maw of such a place as we gathered at the First Baptist Church of Austin. I knew what to expect, but the others probably did not. Jeanne, the third-generation Presbyterian elder, was accustomed to quiet consensus and the formation of committees when conflicts arose. Sara, a prairie Episcopalian, was also used to more genteel leadership by rectors and bishops with remarkable academic pedigrees and long robes. Joy, of course, was a product of a virulent fundamentalism not very different from the kind that threatened Baylor and from the idea of soul competence.

Our host was to be the senior pastor at First Baptist, Roger Paynter. His history was intertwined with many of the people I had known in Baptist life, including Hulitt Gloer, Randall O'Brien, and Todd Lake from Belmont. In Texas, Baptists are often referred to in one of two ways: either "moderate" or "conservative." It apparently is such anathema to the culture that no one identifies as a "liberal." Paynter, like some (but not all) of my Texas friends, fell into the "moderate" category, and his wife, Suzie, had recently been named the executive coordinator of the Cooperative Baptist Fellowship, a group of about 1,800 churches that generally fall under the "moderate" description.

We met Roger when we stumbled into his office at the back of the large church on (appropriately named) Trinity Street in downtown Austin. First, though, we talked to his office manager who had been fielding calls about the trial all week, many driven by a wonderful article on March 23 in the *Austin American-Statesman* in which Juan Castillo described the upcoming event. In one memorable call, an outraged parishioner asked why the church would host a "mockery of Jesus." The office manager explained that in fact it was a "mock trial" of Jesus and how that was a distinct kind of enterprise. After we roundly apologized for putting her through such things, we were off to lunch.

Roger drove past the chain restaurants and took us to an out-of-the-way taqueria with bare tables and a noisy, bustling kitchen. The place was wreathed with the heavenly scent of warm tortillas. We sat at a booth with Roger, sipping ice tea from colored plastic glasses, munching on chips and salsa, and talking. Jeanne soon learned that she also had a connection to Roger: he had been a young seminarian at Southern Baptist Theological Seminary, where Jeanne's pastor and friend Dr. John Boyle had long ago served as chaplain. Boyle had entered the ministry after returning from service in the U.S. Army during WWII, fighting in France and Germany with the 42nd Rainbow Division. Boyle's unit was one of the first to liberate the Nazi concentration camp at Dachau, where Boyle saw horrors that led him to a life of compassion for the suffering.

Paynter recalled a hated task he had been given at the seminary. Because his name rhymed with "painter," an overling with a twisted sense of humor had assigned him the job of painting the rooms in the late summer of hot, muggy Louisville, Kentucky. The rooms were small, with no ventilation, and Paynter felt sick from the fumes. Boyle came by to check on him one day and immediately demanded that fans be installed to help the struggling Paynter breathe. Paynter never forgot that small human gesture.

In his own gentle way, Paynter pressed for an explanation of why we were against the death penalty. I gave my usual arguments, but Jeanne took a different tack and simply told her story (or, in Baptist circles, her "testimony"). One detail fascinated Paynter: the letter that Jeanne received from David Biro, in which he takes responsibility for his crime for the first time and explains his own moral evolution. Jeanne had a copy with her, and Paynter took it eagerly and ignored his food as he began to read it hungrily. We sat in silence. In that moment, I realized what I was witnessing: a minister who had preached for years about forgiveness was digging into the archeology of a remarkable human event.

The event itself built momentum throughout the day. I began to see friends filter in from my past, including former Baylor students like James Nortey, who had gone on to Harvard Law School, where he hosted a talk I gave to a joint gathering of the school's NAACP and Federalist Society chapters. One of my good friends from Waco, Federal Magistrate Judge Jeff Manske, strode in, as did Megan Willome, who had written a profile of me when *Wacoan* magazine named me the "Wacoan of the Year" in 2009 (an honor that unfortunately came not long before I left town for Minnesota). As the crowd swelled into the hundreds and a television crew set up its equipment, I realized the opportunity that we had.

As the crowd gathered, I greeted old friends and chatted with people I didn't know. The latter is not one of my strengths, but I felt emboldened by the crowd and had an important question that needed to be answered: Was this crowd inclined for or against the death penalty? In my short informal poll, the results were mixed—about what you would expect in a "moderate" Baptist church in Austin.

Joy gave our opening, and as she did so, her Texas accent came out strongly. It worked, too, as I watched members of the audience nodding along. Sara gave the opening for the defense, and as usual she offered a strong contrast to Joy's informality. Sara is tall and stands straight like a South Dakota windmill; people hushed when she began.

Peter was played by a member of the congregation with theological training, and I knew that it would be a challenging examination. As the prosecutor, I was allowed to treat him as a hostile witness (as usual), given his ties to the defendant, and used all my training to control what he could say. He clearly was eager to offer more explanation, but I cut him off. For example, when I got him to agree that Jesus had said that people should leave their families to follow him, he said, "Yes, but . . ." and got no further. I had never felt comfortable using this technique, but it is a necessity for prosecutors as they admit facts into evidence and build their case to surpass the threshold of "beyond a reasonable doubt."

Something about the size and grandeur of the space made me subtly shift the emphasis in my closing. I lingered on my description of the threat Jesus posed to heritage and learning. He had, after all, chosen followers like Peter, an illiterate fisherman, while describing the learned people of his time as a "den of vipers." A church like this—much like the schools we had been touring—had been built on a foundation of learning and close examination of the Bible, something Jesus' closest followers would not have been capable of. As I finished up my closing by linking the threat that Jesus posed with his condemnation of riches, I could see the audience eager to begin their discussions. A voice rang out from the back of the church: "Execute him!" The comment was either true to the Gospels (that is what the council called out) or true to Texas. Either way, it fit.

There was to be one more interruption before sentencing, however. As I finished my rebuttal in closing argument, the time came for the judge to read instructions to the jurors—the audience—and tell them to deliberate their verdict. When he did so, however, one man in the audience of about four hundred people startled us by rising to his feet and making a loud announcement: "I need to recuse myself, Your Honor," the man declared. "I'm with Justice for All, and I believe in the death penalty." With that, he strode to the center aisle of the church and out the front door. I knew what that meant: Justice for All was a Houston-based, tough-on-crime organization and one of the nation's staunchest supporters of the death penalty.

Some people look bemused; others, befuddled. There was a low buzzing of voices as the man stalked out of the sanctuary. No one followed him; members of the audience turned to one another and started talking over the case. I did my usual post-trial routine, milling around eavesdropping on the jurors' discussions, surreptitiously snapping pictures. Then I looked up from my camera and saw that someone had followed him: it was Jeanne, strolling up the same aisle taken by the man who had made the loud announcement. I wondered if something was wrong as her gait verged on a run, an unusual urgency for the usually calm defender.

About ten minutes later, I walked out into the soft night and saw the man smoking a cigarette on a porch outside the church and chatting amiably with Jeanne. She stood listening, a warm smile on her face. I approached, shooting her a quizzical look. "Mark, this is a fellow lawyer," Jeanne said, motioning toward me to join them. "I was just thanking him so much for coming."

It turned out that besides being a frequent spokesman and lobbyist for the hard-core, pro-death penalty Justice for All, the man had a law practice, of all things, defending criminals. His specialty was defending drunk drivers. The cigarette in his hand (he had come outside to smoke, not, as we'd thought, to make a grand gesture in rejection of the trial) and the DUI defense card he handed me made him human, not a threat to be feared or an eccentric to be ridiculed. We talked for a while, a cordial conversation. Then it was time to go back inside to collect the jurors' verdicts.

"Wasn't that great?" Jeanne bubbled excitedly, as we walked back in to the church. "Now I know what Jesus was talking about, about the lost sheep." This was typical of conversations with Jeanne, whose mind seemed to be ordered according to her encyclopedic knowledge of the Bible.

"What?" I answered, wondering where this was going.

"That story Jesus told about a shepherd watching a hundred sheep and one leaving the herd. The shepherd leaves the ninety-nine sheep behind and goes after the one. It's not that the one sheep is bad, and the shepherd is going to drag him back to where he ought to be," she said. "It's the shepherd saying to the one sheep, 'You are valuable. You matter. You are worth coming after.' "

Austin at dusk in the spring is a beautiful place—the air is fragrant and soft and warm, and the light is diffuse. A part of me did not want to go back in to hear the verdicts and reengage with the deep, dark vein that ran through our project. I had no choice, though; Roger Paynter was waving us in.

There were two stark differences at First Baptist in the jury verdicts, relative to our previous presentations of the trial. First, one jury actually voted for execution, the first time that had happened. When it was announced, Joy leaned over and whispered, "Told ya'! *Texas*."

The second distinction was rooted in the nature of Texas Baptists, that priesthood of believers where everyone was his or her own favorite theologian (including, of course, myself). No one was able to simply read the result of his or her vote; rather, they all felt compelled to explain, often at length, their reasoning. Many also included criticisms of the presentation itself, such as its infidelity to the actual procedure under Jewish or Roman law at the time. The judge was running the taking of verdicts, and we simply nodded and took notes as each group weighed in. One of the forepersons was James Nortey, my friend who was the recent graduate of Harvard Law. He is the child of Ghanaian immigrants and one of the few black men in the crowd of hundreds. His voice was loud and clear from the back of the room, and succinct; I made a mental note that if we did the trial again in Texas, he would make an excellent judge.

Once the verdicts were done and the questions answered, the four of us scurried to a back room where we had stored a change of clothes and then headed off for dinner with two of the remarkable people from my Sunday school class at Seventh and James, Bob and Mary Darden. Mary is an educator who lives life deeply; later in her career she became the head of a college in San Antonio. Bob, as I often told others, was the person from Baylor who in a hundred years would be seen to have made the most impact.

Bob is a journalism professor who has taught scores of Baylor students how to construct a story and define a character. Many of his students went on to become movie and television writers, and they developed a great tradition. In their scripts, the first person killed is always named "Robert Darden." At this point, poor Bob has been killed off by a Chicago fire, Angelina Jolie, a car wreck, and at least a dozen other misfortunes.

Being killed isn't why Bob will be remembered, though. He will be remembered for saving the legacy of black gospel music. He grew up moving from place to place as his father was moved around by the Air Force, and his one constant was the music he loved. He became a popular writer on the topic, which has also informed his academic work. Most significant, though, he has literally saved the songs themselves. Old vinyl records were decaying in bedrooms and attics across the country, and master tapes of gospel music were rarely preserved. Seeing that his beloved music was literally wasting away, he did what he does best: he wrote about it. In a masterful op-ed in the *New York Times*, he pleaded for someone to preserve this art form in a modern digital format.

It worked. A funder contacted him and provided seed money for Bob to gather old records and hire an archivist. He and Mary traveled the South gathering records, returning to Waco to download the music.

It was a brilliant move and one that reflected his deep passion. I remember one afternoon driving and turning on the radio to hear Bob talking to Terry Gross on NPR's *Fresh Air*, not only explaining the music but playing it for her. Bob's archives, rooted in his long drives with Mary across Alabama, Mississippi, and Tennessee, are now becoming a part of the Smithsonian's National Museum of African American History and Culture.

These were our guides as we walked a few blocks over to Stubb's Barbecue, the legendary Austin food joint and music venue. We sat at a long wooden table, drank good beer, and laughed at it all. Bob and Mary were in their element and clearly loved the company. Stories were told, and another round was ordered.

There are not enough moments of joy like that. When they happen, I try to drink it in and appreciate each bit. As I looked around at my friends, I knew that for each of them their laughter was a transcendence of some deep inner pain. Sara still mourned the loss of her mother, and Joy the loss of her family in a different way. Jeanne was reliving the death of her sister as she began to confront the human reality of Nancy's killer. "Only I," I thought to myself, "haven't felt that weight of unjust loss." Just me. I looked down and traced a letter carved into the table with the tip of my finger, for just that moment not hearing the laughter or the warmth in the voices of my friends.

Stephen Osler, Easter
(photo courtesy of Mark Osler; used by permission)

Chapter 13

Louisiana

*T*here were over seven months between our trial at First Baptist Austin and the next performances in Louisiana. There was no lull in our worlds, though. By this time, Joy had moved to Minnesota and was sharing a house with Sara and her family. Later, all of them would move to Chicago, leaving me as the only regular cast member not living in that city.

Jeanne was especially busy. She had begun a remarkable project, the culmination of her changing ideas about forgiveness. She had begun to visit David Biro in prison and was writing a book that chronicled all that had happened before and after Randall O'Brien challenged her thinking about what forgiveness and reconciliation meant to a Christian. In a way, that writing was a return to her roots. She was trained as a writer at one of the nation's best schools— Northwestern University's Medill School of Journalism—before taking a different tangent and going on to law school. Now, for the first time in thirty years, she was a writer again.

My own life was in transition as well. My son Micah was entering his senior year in high school, and it was time to take him on a college tour. The plan was to swing through Chicago, visit my parents in Detroit, and then head east. It's a bittersweet gift for a parent to have that time with a beloved child who is about to leave home. As we drove, we talked about the events of his life and his thoughts on his own future. He asked about my work, and I told him the good and the bad, describing the dark place I inhabited when I stood before a church and argued against the value of Christ. He listened attentively. We did not need the radio.

As we closed in on Detroit, we decided to take a short detour in Ann Arbor to see my brother Will. His wife, Kim, was at work, but when I called, Will was at home with his kids. They live in a beautiful old neighborhood not far from Zingerman's Deli, in a white wood-frame house that is older than anyone we know. Because Will and Kim are musicians, their home is full of instruments, and it is rare to go in and out without doing a little singing.

As we walked up to the house, Will came to the door and gave me a welcoming hug as his daughter, Alexa, and his son, Stephen, ran up. The cousins are close, and Micah has always been the ringleader when they gather. As we sat in the living room catching up, Micah asked if he could play the piano. That is his habit, as he can't resist a vacant piano bench. Will nodded agreeably, and Micah started banging out "Bohemian Rhapsody," which he had recently taught himself to play. Stephen looked on eagerly and loved the raucousness of the song as it rang through the house. As we left, Stephen followed us to the door of the car with perhaps a new appreciation for his eldest cousin. They both loved loud, bold music.

That wasn't the major trip of my summer, though. St. Thomas has a summer program in Rome, and I had been asked to teach there. It seemed a great opportunity, and I jumped at the chance to teach a six-week course in comparative criminal law. By the middle of June I was ensconced in a small apartment in Trastevere above a tiny store run by an old lady who was helped by a boy who came and went on a motor scooter painted in the colors of the Italian flag.

Though my students were wonderful and energetic, Rome was a hard place for me. As it had been (on and off) for some two thousand years, it was crowded and dirty, and I found myself homesick. The problem was more my fault than Rome's, though; I was a silent introvert in a city of gregarious people. New York is different, a city of introverts forced to live together, which makes them interact in artful ways. I like that. I know how to do that. Rome, where people talk to strangers for no reason at all, is alien territory. They will dash into a "snack bar" to get an espresso and drink it standing up at the counter, talking to whoever else is there in a mad flurry of words. That's not me—I'm the guy sitting in the brown, soft chair at Starbucks, keeping to himself and finishing some work on his laptop.

That meant that I spent a lot of time reading in the odd little apartment and a lot more wandering alone through the bustling city, lonely in the middle of a crowd. I would cross the Tibur at dusk, pass through the Campo di Fiori, loop by the Piazza Navona, then go past the Pantheon toward places unknown before trying to find my way back. In each piazza there would be musicians, cafes, and groups of men selling a certain little toy that was popular that summer: a small rocket you could shoot into the air; it would then propeller back down to earth, glowing light blue like a shooting star.

The vendors were good at shooting them up, and the arc of the toy's return was graceful, casting a faint light onto the gods of Bernini's public sculptures. It was their best sales tool, and they did it constantly. You could tell where one of the big piazzas was located from a few blocks away just by looking for the light of these spinning angels gently returning to earth. They were good at having the rocket come straight back to their hands, but most people lost them right away as they shot off onto a rooftop or ledge.

One night as I slept in my bed just a few dozen yards from the Tibur, the phone rang. I jumped up and looked at the clock; it was 4 a.m. I panicked as I clambered out of my loft bed and searched for the phone. I knew that nothing good was conveyed in a call at four in the morning and hoped it was simply a wrong number.

Grabbing my phone too late to answer, I saw that the call was from my parents. For a moment I sat, looking at it. If they were calling, that probably meant that at least nothing bad had happened to them. I breathed in and out to calm myself and called them back. When they told me, together, what had happened, my calm was over, and the world went dark.

My brother and his son, Stephen, had been canoeing in Lake Michigan during a camping trip to the Sleeping Bear Dunes. They were like that, a father and son who loved to enjoy the outdoors together. Will was a responsible and experienced canoeist, and he made sure they had life jackets on and a good plan for their trip. The boat capsized when hit with a huge wave, however, and it couldn't be righted. When he realized they were in trouble, Will used his cell phone (carefully sealed into a zippered bag) to call for help. When that help finally came hours later, both father and son were close to death of exposure. Will survived. Stephen, the boy with a song in his heart, did not.

The day my parents called about Stephen's death, I told my students what had happened. They were ashen and silent. They were close enough to children themselves, closer to his eight years old than to my fifty. They understood that I had to go home to Detroit. Their lives in Trastevere would go on as before, a cycle of reading and drinking and walking and reading about the rolling series of tragedies that is criminal law.

It turned out that there was a flight between Detroit and Rome, a nonstop that takes off over the Roman ruins at Ostia and lands over the American ruins of Henry Ford's Rouge plant. When I explained to the airline what had happened, they got me a seat on that flight, and I packed up a few things and left the brown of Rome for the gray of Detroit.

Detroit is, like Rome, a city most notable for what used to be. You drive by a crumbling wall and point and talk about what was once there and imagine what it was like when it was a church or a factory or a mansion. It's a good place to go to be sad, to mourn, because that is the nature of it. There are no toy rockets in the night sky, no crowds in the street on a random Tuesday, no one standing in front of a cafe urging you in. When people hear that someone is from Detroit, sometimes they think he must be tough or dangerous, but usually it just means he is carrying a sad secret.

Coming in from the airport in my parents' old minivan, I saw what I always see: nothing where there used to be something. Rome went from being a million people at its height to under 60,000 in the Dark Ages; Detroit went from nearly two million to under 700,000 now. What that leaves are spaces in the dark where there used to be people and things and life. My mother, in her grief, still pointed out the pretty wildflowers that grew in a broad, flat lot where houses and a supermarket used to be. She is the kind of person who sees beauty everywhere. I'm not, though; as we drive through what comes to my mind is the book of Lamentations, which says,

How lonely sits the city
  that once was full of people!
How like a widow she has become,
  she that was great among the nations!
                        (Lam. 1:1)

Ruins don't just appear. Both Detroit and Rome were looted and
burned. I was there for one of them. I was very young but just old
enough to remember it. We were kept in, of course, during the riots,
but that just makes a small child want to run outside and see what
was happening, and that is what I did.

Once outside, I saw something that changed me. The U. S. Army
had occupied the city—not just the reserves, but the active duty guys
coming from or going to Vietnam—and I saw some small part of it,
a jeep or an armored personnel carrier or a soldier. There was something about that sight that terrified me. I knew there was a war somewhere and also that something was wrong in the city, but now it all
became clear in the way of a four-year-old who sees the whole world
as his block: the war was in my city. And then the city was gone, at
least to me, and we lived in a new house in a new town where the
parents didn't play volleyball at dusk.

When I returned to Rome after the service for Stephen, I started
to see angels. There are the artists' angels, of course—the archan-
gels and putti everywhere. In frescoes, they are advising, celebrating,
consoling, conspiring. In a church not far from my classroom I found
the angel Gabriel, telling Mary of her fate. It is not a celebration but
a consolation; the angel holds out one hand, about to touch Mary's
shoulder, her face full of concern. He is reaching out to someone
getting troubling news. That, I thought, was the angel who had been
there the night my parents called.

There is a bridge from Trastevere over the Tibur near that fresco
of Gabriel and Mary, the Ponte Sisto. It is old and timeworn and
looks a little unreliable. It is blocked off for pedestrians, one of
the few parts of Rome that is. Elsewhere, even on the narrowest of
streets, a car will appear and nudge pedestrians to the wall. Not on
the Ponte Sisto, though. It is a haven for people with nowhere to go,
who may or may not be selling something. A hippie couple with their
dog might be asleep by the wall; Rastafarians could be banging on

drums; or a busload of American high school students might be snapping pictures on any given night.

My last evening in Rome, after I had gathered my things to leave
for good, I walked over the Ponte Sisto toward the Campo di Fiori.
It was a warm night, and the bridge was full of people. For once, I
acted like a Roman. I walked slowly; I talked to people; I stood for a
while and just watched the light over the river and eavesdropped on
couples. Someone offered me a cigarette, and I demurred in Italian,
the first time I had tried that with a stranger.

At the piazza, people were beginning to gather. I took a table for
one at the edge of the square, ordered fish and wine, and watched
them all. A woman waited for someone, wearing a pink dress and
tennis shoes, furtively checking her makeup in a small mirror. Kids
climbed on top of a car as an old man yelled at them from a window.
At the bar next door, American college kids began to gather and
laugh as the dusk arrived.

As I finished my dinner, I realized what I needed. I walked into
the piazza and tracked one of the little starlight rockets down to its
salesman, a small man with a bag slung over his shoulder. He was
not Italian, but I had no idea where he was from, only the certainty
that it was someplace far away where there was little work. As I
approached, he turned toward a family with two little boys. The technique of selling these things is easy; you find a way to get one into a
child's hand, and the parent is on the hook. It didn't work with this
family, though. The dad barked at the vendor in German and walked
on, and when the vendor turned back, I approached him.

"How much are they?" I asked. There was a pause, one I had
become used to, where two people without a common language
begin a discussion. Each of us was evaluating the situation. There
was a lot of pantomime involved.

He looked behind me pointedly, then to either side, then back at
me. "Child?" he asked. "For toy?"

A longer pause. "There is no child," I murmured. Dumbly, I motioned
to the blank space behind me. "No . . . child." Then I started to cry.

In that still, small moment, he knew. He looked at me with complete understanding. Where he was from, children died. They died
of diseases we cured a long time ago, got hit by fast cars on bad
roads, and got shot in wars. They died in ways we cannot imagine.

They died from drinking water. He looked at me with sympathy and reached out his hand, the palm up. "*Cosa e successo?*" he asked.

I knew what he meant, what it was he wanted. We introverts, scared of words, get good at that. He wanted to know how the boy had died.

"He was eight," I told him. "They went canoeing on Lake Michigan, and the canoe capsized. He was wearing a life jacket, but it took too long to get there, too long to find them." I stopped crying. It was good to tell the story. "He loved to sing, and he was so smart." I looked out at the angels descending and bit my lip. "So smart."

He nodded at me and reached into his bag. He pulled out one of the tiny rockets, handed it to me, and then put his hands up to refuse payment. I did an awkward bow of thanks and walked off. The next day I flew off, back to Minnesota and a familiar certainty I craved.

Nothing was the same, though. I longed to do something, the right thing, for my brother, but I didn't know what that would be. It's hard to be the big brother, the one who picks his sibling up off of the ice and dusts him off when a tragedy seems bigger than God. I called and wrote and came back to Michigan, but I felt awkward and fumbling and inadequate. I am a word person, but there are times, I suppose, when there are no words.

Back in Minnesota I had to steel myself for the gauntlet I had constructed for that autumn, even as I woke up every morning thinking of my brother and his son struggling in cold water. I was scheduled to give public lectures in Savannah, Georgia; at William and Mary; in Anchorage, Alaska; at Stanford Law School; at UCLA Law School; at Harvard Law School; and at Loyola Marymount; and to give sermons in three different states. All this was on top of teaching sentencing and running my clemency clinic. At the start of the semester, I sat at my desk for nearly an hour one morning, unable to open up my calendar. I was overwhelmed.

Then I opened my mail.

Thousands of people, mostly black men, sat in federal prison doing lengthy terms for nonviolent drug offenses involving crack. Many of them would be out by now under the current law, but Congress had not made reforms enacted in 2010 retroactive. Dozens of them wrote to me, hoping that we could help them get clemency. Their letters usually came in brown, rectangular, letter-sized envelopes, with the prisoner ID number carefully included in the return address.

For a week or more at the start of that semester, those letters sat and waited for me to gather the emotional energy to read them. I knew from experience what I would find in most of those brown envelopes: a polite plea for help and a plaintive description of compounded tragedies. Often they would include documents, and I would read a transcript or appellate brief that revealed a system that was harsh and arbitrary, far beyond what safety required. I had been reading the book Joanne Braxton had given me, Ernest Gaines's *A Lesson before Dying*. It was gripping and sad, and I now understood why my mentor had slipped it to me like a jewel in a velvet bag. The pain in the book was the pain in the letters I received. In one passage, a young man about to be executed cries out for the black hero of his day: "Help me, Joe Louis! Help me!" I was no Joe Louis and felt unworthy of my own mail.

Then something happened. A reporter, Abby Rapoport, was visiting me in my office. She was a writer for *American Prospect*, and I knew her father—Ron Rapoport, my beloved professor at William and Mary—and her grandparents who lived in Waco. At a break in our interview, I opened one of the long, brown envelopes. It was from a federal prisoner in Texas named Ronald Blount, who was serving a life sentence without the possibility of parole. Abby returned text messages as I opened the envelope.

Quickly, I glanced through the contents, which included a short letter, the transcript of his sentencing hearing, and the presentence report prepared by a court officer prior to the sentencing. The first thing I turned to, at random, was a short passage where Mr. Blount was responding to the judge's question about his role in a crack-selling business:

The Defendant: I mean, they said—and you heard—I took them to this place over there to obtain—

The Court: Where they got crack.

The Defendant: They got it from the village where I hang at. I hang at a store begging for nickels and quarters and dimes. I stayed on the front porch of my mama's house, man. I don't even have one change of clothes. I had to wash every day, Judge. How can I be a seller of dope?

It seemed like it couldn't be true—this impoverished addict receiving a life term. I quickly turned to the presentence investigation report, which offers an important level of objectivity. Shockingly, it just confirmed what Mr. Blount had said in court: that he was an addict; that he had very low-level involvement in the operation, mostly consisting of telling customers where to go to buy crack; and that he did live on his mother's porch. The life sentence he received was intended for drug kingpins who made themselves wealthy on the drug trade. Something had gone terribly wrong.

I put the brown envelope in my bag to carry with me as I traveled, and I assigned two of my students to begin working on the case with copies of the materials he had sent. I could not save Stephen or even console my brother, but perhaps I could help Ronald Blount. That brown envelope, by now a totem of my mission, was in my weathered, green canvas bag as I went to Virginia, Alaska, California, and Massachusetts that fall. It was also with me as I landed at Louis Armstrong International Airport in New Orleans in November, not far from the Lake Charles Courthouse where Ronald Blount had been given his life sentence.

A Jesuit priest was my guide to the city, and soon he took me to Loyola University, where we were to perform the trial. New Orleans is perhaps the most haunted and intriguing of American cities, but I took little notice of its mysteries as I met up with Jeanne and those we would work with on the performance. We each adopted a law student there as our second chair, and my new partner was a sharp-eyed Minnesotan, a third-year student in a red dress named Kara Larson. She was eager to get to work, and later as our witnesses arrived, I was glad to see her preparing earnestly. My own heart did not feel so invested; there was a lack of color in everything.

The room filled up with students and faculty; it appeared that some of the students had been assigned to attend as a part of class. Jeanne and her student partner were talking with U.S. District Court Judge Helen Berrigan, who would preside, and a group of professors. As the room filled up, I was holed away with my old red Bible, finding a few new citations to use. Suddenly, I felt the fire of the moment, the strongest emotion I had allowed myself in months, and once we began, I realized that everything was different. In the previous trials, there was deep cognitive dissonance in denouncing Jesus, but somehow my condemnations came naturally, without conflict. I *was* angry at God.

The new citations that I had dug up fit my new mood. For the first time, I used the full text of Matthew 10:34–36, where Jesus says,

> "Do not think that I have come to bring peace to the earth; I have not come to bring peace, but a sword.
> For I have come set a man against his father,
> and a daughter against her mother,
> . . . .
> and one's own foes will be members of one's own household."

As I brought that passage into evidence through Peter, reading it verbatim, I felt the cruel edge of it deep in my soul, the awful heartlessness of a savior with a sword. Previously, I had excised the first part, about the sword, but now I was willing to put it into play, to recognize that dark majestic vision.

I then moved quickly to something else new to the trial, from Matthew 8:21–22: "Another of his disciples said to him, 'Lord, first let me go and bury my father.' But Jesus said to him, 'Follow me, and let the dead bury their own dead.'"

"So this is your Master?" I railed at the poor student playing Peter, breaking my own discipline with cross-examination. "The one with the sword, the one who tells his follower not to return to his own dead father?"

In my closing, the emotion only intensified. I leaned into it and talked about the dangerous Jesus, the one who promised the sword and then delivered it—who allowed the slave Malchus to be cut before healing him in a showy "miracle" and then return to a lifetime of abject servitude. It was strangely exhilarating. For a moment, I was able to displace my own deep sadness with this anger I had welling up in me, an anger at a creation of God where Stephen's voice was stilled, where an addict rots in prison while a kingpin rests in luxury, where a killer shoots a pregnant woman in the stomach, and where Katherine Darmer falls from a parking garage, a world awash in tragedy and death. It was very real. For the first time, I was calling for the blood of Jesus, and I meant it.

When we finished, I felt a strange calm come over me. I wanted to talk to Joy, but she was not there with us. I finally understood her words at the Loud Dinner. The others were gathered around the judge, so I slipped outside as I often did during deliberations.

New Orleans is full of water. Water is held back by the levees, engorges the river, and is heavy in the air all around. As I stepped out into that watery world, it was as though I was being baptized into anger, and I felt the urge to let out a guttural wolf-like howl of something more naked than sad helplessness. Suddenly the landscape fit me, and I reveled in it. The languid trees spread their branches horizontally, draped with moss, clouding the sightlines in every direction. Something about it fed the primal impulse I had unleashed, the abject disgust at the pain and injustice God allowed.

Back inside, the world was normal. The students, with varying level of interest, discussed the case as jurors. The judge and Jeanne and the faculty members stood in a tight circle and talked about the death penalty. My rage had not unbalanced the whole of it, but it was noticeable and perhaps strangely effective. The next day, Jarvis DeBerry wrote about it in the New Orleans *Times-Picayune*:

> Still, putting Jesus on trial seemed at first a cutesy gimmick, unlikely to persuade the stalwart who believes the worst among us should be irreversibly removed from the rest of us. But there was something about Osler's presentation, the way he relentlessly pressed his case against the defendant that made me glad I wasn't on a jury. Because I may have voted for death.
>
> That's not because I'm a death penalty supporter. I'm not. But if I had sworn to follow the law and heard a prosecutor making a case like this one was, what could I have done but vote for death?
>
> And that, it occurred to me, was the point of the exercise. Many of us revere the law more than we revere life itself. We don't let our consciences interfere when authorities point out what's written on the books. We go along with things we feel are wrong because we're told that what we feel is irrelevant.[1]

I read DeBerry's article as we traveled with the priest to our next stop, St. George's Catholic Church in Baton Rouge, and was happy

---

1. Jarvis DeBerry, "Death Penalty Opponents Put 'Jesus on Trial,'" *Times-Picayune* (Nov. 8, 2013), http://www.nola.com/opinions/index.ssf/2013/11/death_penalty_opponents _put_je.html.

that my performance had received that generous and probably undeserved perception.

In a few hours we were in Baton Rouge, wandering the parking lots that surrounded St. George's. It was a largely Hispanic congregation lodged in a big modern building near a street thick with fast-food restaurants and strip malls. As we surveyed the stage, I was wondering if the trial would again unleash that deep anger, which seemed barely at bay. However, here there was something different. Instead of the somewhat impassive students at Loyola, our audience was composed of family groups and people who had on a mixture of church clothes and work clothes. They were not assigned to come; they were there because of the imperatives of faith and the hard questions it brings.

My edge was gone, but Jeanne was changed. She had, I suppose, seen the rage inside of me. Perhaps more than anyone I worked with, she understood it. I later found an interview she did with the *Chicago Reader*, where Robert McClory wrote about her reaction to the death of her sister: "Bishop says her first reaction to the tragedy was anger and confusion. 'I was mad at God. I wondered what good prayer was, why God didn't intervene to stop evil.' "[2] There had been a time that she had felt the same way I did, but that wasn't where she was anymore. In Baton Rouge, she redoubled her plea for compassion as an ethic and as an action, telling the jury in her closing, "No one is beyond the redemption of God. No one is beyond the purpose of God. Then how can we have a death penalty?" I sat at the other table and watched her. I should have been gathering my notes for rebuttal, but instead I was thinking that she had stated a theology that was as whole and countercultural as any I had heard. For the first time in months, I was hearing and thinking again. The rage had unblocked something within me.

We finished early in the evening, and the crowd dissipated into the haze of Sunday traffic on the busy street nearby. A few of us stood outside saying our good-byes. There was a line of tall trees, and then the parking lots and road beyond. I knew that this was where Sister Helen Prejean was from, a middle-class girl who became a crusader

---

2. Robert McClory, "Full Pardon, *Chicago Reader,* January 16, 1997, http://www.chicago reader.com/chicago/full-pardon/Content?oid=892491.

against the death penalty and the bold woman I had first seen walking arm in arm with Jeanne Bishop that day in Atlanta. Something had changed Helen Prejean and transformed her into the New Orleans nun who both worked with the poor and coerced governors after seeing the worst that people can do to one another. People change. Perhaps I could, too.

I jammed my notes and Bible into the green canvas bag, and there was the letter from Ronald Blount. As prisoners often do, he had put too many stamps on it, far more than were necessary. One stamp bore a picture of the Statue of Liberty. Three said, "Justice"; four said, "Equality"; and one said, "Liberty." I knew that in prison, a single stamp could be bought with about one hour of wages. Ronald Blount had worked for nine hours just to buy the stamps for that envelope. Once he had done so, he had sent it to me. Now it was mine to carry with me like a cross. And, with that, the wolf was gone; the hunting was done; and the humid air was still and quiet.

Gordon Davenport and Mark Osler outside
Grace-St. Paul Episcopal Church, Tucson
(photo courtesy of Martha Witaker; used by permission)

Chapter 14

Tucson

Asking someone from Minnesota to come to Tucson in February is a pretty high-percentage shot, and when that invitation came from an old friend, I grabbed it. I was unsure if any of my collaborators could join me, but when the snow was deep by my front door, saying yes was an instinctive reaction.

New projects meant that the trial was nearing the end of its course. Jeanne and I were being pulled in different directions by the same powerful force. We had both begun—each for our own reason—to try to live out Christ's directive in Matthew 25 that when we visit those in prison, we visit him. It is a challenging passage for criminal lawyers, as the murderer becomes the savior, and the defendant's annoying mother who calls the defense lawyer every day becomes Mary. As our paths diverged, Jeanne and I each found our way to prison and the people inside. For Jeanne, the prisoner was David Biro, who had killed her pregnant sister and brother-in-law. For me, it was the men and women who sent me those large brown envelopes asking me to help.

David Biro had killed Jeanne's sister but never taken responsibility for it. For years, his intransigence had made it impossible for her to reconcile with him in any meaningful way. In 1997, she told the *Chicago Reader*, "I believe in the possibility of redemption for every human being. But how do you reconcile with a person who says he didn't do it?"[1] Bishop's book, *Change of Heart*, explains

---

1. Robert McCLory, "Full Pardon: Murder, Revenge, and the Power of Forgiveness," *Chicago Reader*, January 16, 1997.

how eventually she did exactly that. It began, contrary to expectation, with her apologizing first:

> I had spoken about the murders and forgiveness all over the world: France, Ireland, Mongolia, Japan, and all across the United States. I had written about forgiving David Biro, given speeches at churches and schools and conferences. The one person I hadn't told: him. Never once had I communicated my forgiveness to David Biro.
> I had waited all these years for him to apologize to me. I saw it now with startling clarity: I had to apologize to him, for never telling him that I had forgiven him. I had to go first.[2]

And so she did, writing him a letter. She wrote boldly, apologizing for her failure to reach out and slipping it into the blue mailbox near her home in Winnetka, Illinois.

Not long after, we were preparing to present the trial in one of its 2012 iterations. I was busy with my notes and my Bible when she interrupted with an envelope in her hand—a familiar brown rectangular letter like the one from Ronald Blount. She was shaking as she handed it to me, unopened, and I saw the return address: Pontiac Prison in Illinois. The letter was from David Biro. Jeanne had called a few days before and asked if I could read it before she did, and that moment had come.

Jeanne Bishop is no fragile flower. Her job requires a steely toughness that few possess; she literally has to go into some of America's worst jails and prisons, sit down alone with violent felons, and negotiate with them. Sometimes she has to talk them into going to trial (if they are innocent) or taking a fair plea deal (if they are guilty), angering a violent man whose strong tattooed arms are only a few inches away from her in the cramped attorney meeting room. I had never seen her betray an ounce of fear in the face of the harshest criticism or angriest supporter of retribution, but now she was different. She had staked her hopes for the redemptive power of forgiveness to the sealed envelope in my hand. I knew that if she had the chance she would search my face for clues as I read, so I made up an errand and

---

2. Jeanne Bishop, *Change of Heart: Justice, Mercy, and Making Peace with My Sister's Killer* (Louisville, KY: Westminster John Knox Press, 2015), 95 .

sent her out, and then I stole away and made sure the others did not interrupt me.

I sat outside and held the envelope tightly in my hand. I knew that the contents could be crushing and terrible, a screed of bile and hatred. It felt heavy and thick, after all. I slit the top of the long envelope swiftly, took a breath, and then slid out fifteen carefully numbered pages of orderly handwriting. On the first page, I saw this: "I think the time has come to drop the charade and finally be honest. You're right, I am guilty of killing your sister, Nancy, and her husband, Richard. I also want to take this opportunity to express my deepest condolences and apologize to you." I breathed out and closed my eyes for a moment.

Not long after I finished, Jeanne returned with a plastic bag holding ginger ale and lip balm (I had made up the shopping list on the fly). I looked up and said, "It's good." As I read the letter to her, I heard a deep, honest sob as I got to his confession. This strong, world-changing woman was finally whole.

From that moment, Jeanne had embarked on a renewed journey of hope. She began to visit Biro in prison and to write the book that tells the story of that reconciliation. Though she did not advocate for Biro's release, she did become an important voice against the sentence of life without parole as applied to juvenile offenders— the sentence Biro had received. Her schedule became crowded as the power of her story became known.

My own work went in a different direction, as I redoubled my efforts to revive the Constitutional pardon power as a principled tool of the president. I worked both at retail, creating petitions like Ronald Blount's with my students, and at wholesale, to make the federal clemency system functional again after decades of abuse and neglect by successive presidents. As a prosecutor, the pardon of Marc Rich by Bill Clinton had infuriated me—it ran against any articulable principle. Yet at the same time this crucial presidential power went unused in areas where it could do great good.

I had become fascinated with the actions of President Ford, who quietly created a "Presidential Clemency Board" outside of the Department of Justice in 1974, which was to complete its work within one year and then disband. Their task was to address some twenty-one thousand requests for clemency from Vietnam-era draft evaders and Army deserters. They finished their work on time and were responsible for almost fifteen thousand clemencies. It struck me that the Ford program could be a model both for a short-term project—to clear out the backlog of over-sentenced drug cases—and as a replacement systemically for the inefficient DOJ-based Pardon Office.

With the help of the Open Society Foundation's Nkechi Taifa (a woman largely responsible for the reform of crack laws), I met four times with administration officials to urge a short-term project using the pardon power in a vigorous way. President Obama responded, though not with the Ford Clemency Board approach, and created the Clemency Project 2014, which availed the help of advocacy groups instead. Next, in pursuing a long-term fix, I collaborated with NYU professor and U.S. Sentencing Commissioner Rachel Barkow. We, too, met with administration officials but also wrote an op-ed in the *Washington Post* and an academic article for the *University of Chicago Law Review* that became the basis for a lead editorial in the *New York Times*. My plate was full.

Still, there was time to go to Tucson. I knew three people in that town, and they all conspired to bring the trial there. Hank Shea, my colleague at St. Thomas and the judge for several versions of the trial, had begun spending half the year there in a house he and his wife, Chris, built on a mountainside overlooking the broad valley. He was also teaching at the University of Arizona College of Law, where sentencing scholar Marc Miller had become the dean.

The second person I knew in Tucson was one of my favorite former students, Gordon Davenport. He had graduated from Baylor Law in the first half of my tenure there, and we had remained friends and collaborators afterward. Plus, in a pinch he had served as a babysitter. Gordon is a large person and a skilled litigator who had gotten a coveted position as a federal prosecutor in the Sun Belt.

Finally, one of the more intriguing people from my childhood was Martha Whitaker, who was in the class behind me in high school. She was both an ace student and a champion runner, and our friendship circles overlapped. Her father was an Episcopal priest devoted to social justice; he served both affluent Grosse Pointers and a smaller church in Detroit. Martha had gotten a PhD, married, and taught hydrology at the University of Arizona. She also was the senior warden at Grace-St. Paul's Episcopal Church near campus, where we were to do the trial.

When Martha reached out to me after three decades, having heard about the trial, I was in turn fascinated by her own work. Being a hydrologist in the desert was a compelling job description. It made sense, though: it is the things that are scarcest and most valuable that we must understand the most. In New Orleans, it seemed like water (and the spirits all around) were always in danger of overflowing the walls and destroying the city. I remembered it saturating the air to baptize my anger. In Tucson, though, the danger came from the water that wasn't there.

Martha was curious about the concept of the trial and wanted to know where the idea had come from. Oddly, it was a new question to me, and I stumbled a little with the answer. "We just made it up because it needed to be done," I ended up telling her. It was only in that moment that the unusual nature of the project became clear to me, perhaps because it was coming to a close, as we all seemed to realize.

In preparing for the Tucson version of the trial, I found that Arizona law was different from that of other states. Instead of following trial orthodoxy, the capital proceeding there is divided into three parts rather than two. First guilt is determined; then an aggravating factor is found; and then a sentence is imposed. Most challenging for our purposes, the sentencing phase there allowed for an unusual process where victim testimony comes first, followed by defense evidence. We were going to have to change our presentation significantly to fit the state law.

I wrote to Gordon Davenport, who was going to serve as my second chair. As a federal prosecutor, Gordon already had a wealth of trial experience and spoke with the efficiency seasoned trial attorneys favor. Under the unusual Arizona procedure, we would get only one key witness, and it had to be a "victim" of the crime Jesus was convicted of: blasphemy. "We can't call God," Gordon said definitively.

But who else was hurt by Jesus' power and teaching? As I pondered this question, I was sitting at home in Minnesota in front of a fire as the snow fell outside. In my lap was my old red Bible, which had to hold the answer. I opened to the Gospels and began to search through the now-familiar stories. Almost immediately, I happened upon a perfect fit. "Peter's wife!" I said out loud. My son John, sitting nearby, looked startled.

The passage I had chanced on was Matthew 8, where Jesus travels to Peter's house and finds Peter's mother-in-law lying in bed with a fever. Jesus touches her hand, and she is healed. While the miracle of healing is interesting, what caught my eye was the reference to Peter's mother-in-law: it meant that Peter was married! Moreover, it meant that Peter was married to a woman who must have been virtually abandoned as her husband traveled constantly with Jesus. In that same chapter, Jesus identifies himself as homeless in saying, "'Foxes have holes, and birds of the air have nests; but the Son of Man has nowhere to lay his head'" (v. 20). And there was our victim of Christ's power. I gathered up some lighter clothes from the back of my closet as I packed, wondering how the new witness would play out.

I needn't have worried. At the trial at Martha's Episcopal church, Gordon examined the woman playing Peter's wife masterfully. I felt some pride as I watched him, as I was one of his many teachers, and he had learned well. First he laid the groundwork and had her describe their life together, when Peter worked as a fisherman and they built a home with children together. Next, allowing her to bring drama to the moment, he had her describe the strange appearance of Jesus and the sudden disappearance of Peter, who left her without money or help. It had never occurred to me that the apostles left their families. It should have, though: Jesus explicitly recognizes this in Matthew 19, where he tells his followers that "'everyone who has left houses or brothers or sisters or father or mother or children or fields, for my name's sake, will receive a hundredfold, and will inherit eternal life'" (v. 29). It's a jarring Gospel reality for those who view the family as a key Christian institution.

Our audience was a fascinating mix of academics, snowbirds, family groups, and retired people. As Gordon continued the examination, I watched them as they listened and saw furrowed brows and looks of concern. As we intended, they were troubled.

I gave the closing, with less anger this time. As we waited for the juries to form in a nearby meeting room, I watched Gordon answer questions. The parishioners were naturally drawn to him, and that made sense; he was warm and gregarious and smart. Like Joy, he was a native Texan and bore comfortably the innate sociability of a Texan. As he handled the questions, I stepped outside into the dry night air. Tucson is surrounded by mountains on every side, and in the fading light I could see their rough outline silhouetted against the deep blue of the desert sky. A few stars appeared. It was a gentle night.

After the verdicts came in (more findings of life in prison), the audience wanted to know more about Jeanne's story, and she began to discuss the book she was then completing. She talked about David Biro as a killer but also as someone who still existed, who woke up in the morning and ate, who now was challenged with confronting what he had done. It was a remarkable story arc, and as she spoke, Jeanne formed the shapes of it in the air with her hands as people leaned forward in their chairs. Something subtle had happened; Jeanne now was speaking as an author rather than a lawyer. It was what she was born to do.

In the fall of 2012, as we did the trial four times in a whirlwind of activity, I had been consumed thinking about new witnesses or lines of argument to bring to the project. When I woke up during those months, I was thinking about the Gospel stories of Jesus that I was still learning, these fascinating counterintuitive tales of grace and miracles. It was like Jesus had walked into my life and introduced himself, and I was figuring out what that meant.

Now, though, just as Jeanne likely woke up thinking about the complicated reconciliation with David Biro, I woke up thinking about the people in prison for whom I was writing clemency petitions. It's a remarkable process that is deeply spiritual. A clemency petition is addressed to the president of the United States, and in the end it is that one elected person's judgment that will come to bear. The petition itself, at its heart, tells the life story of the defendant— a story that involves both tragedy and victory. When a petition is completed, I would put it in a large brown envelope, address it to the president, and wait for the most powerful person in the world to decide the fate of the least powerful. Just as I took a breath of hope before I opened that envelope from David Biro, I took a breath of hope each time I sealed an envelope for the White House.

Instead of Jesus and the woman at the well, now I was thinking about Weldon Angelos, who had received a fifty-five-year sentence for a first offense of selling about $1,000 worth of marijuana while possessing (not using or brandishing, just possessing) a firearm. I was thinking about Ronald Blount, who was working in the prison chapel and would call me every Friday, and about Homar Fajardo, whose wife, Marie, waited patiently for the return of a man so safe that the Bureau of Prisons arranged for him to get a driver's license so that he can drive himself to off-site HVAC jobs contracted to prison labor.

The Jesus I see in the Gospels, after all, did not tell us to go to the hungry, the sick, the naked, and those in prison and to show no mercy as we judged their acts. Instead, we are to bring food to the hungry, healing to the sick, clothes to the naked, and hope to those who are in prison. My passion had pivoted in the direction it was pushed. Putting my hands to work had helped to heal my anger at God. There was injustice in the world around me, and I began to understand not only the nature of some of that injustice but the role I played in creating it as I had followed a law that too often allowed for no mercy or humanity. Now I saw: It's not God who creates injustice. We do.

Kent McKeever, Joy Tull, and Mark Osler
at the Sonic in Manchaka, Texas
(photo courtesy of Jeanne Bishop; used by permission)

Chapter 15

Manchaca, Texas

On the wall of my dining room in Minnesota is a beautiful framed map. It was given to me as thanks for a lecture I gave on sentencing in Austin in 2005. The image is familiar to many Texans: it shows the claimed borders of the republic of Texas after the victory at San Jacinto in 1836. Some of the borders—the Gulf coast and the Red River—are familiar, but the republic is shown as extending to the Rocky Mountains, up to and including part of what is now Colorado. It reminds me of the maps that fascinated me as a kid, the ones in history textbooks that show the peak extent of the Roman Empire or the Mongol reign. They are outlines of power.

There are ways, of course, in which that map is still correct. Texas is even bigger than its current broad borders in terms of its influence on our politics and culture. In no area is that more true than the death penalty, where Texas's enthusiasm for capital punishment defines our nation to the world. We needed to go back to Texas, and we needed to get out of Austin, the progressive donut hole in a very conservative state.

Out of the blue, the opportunity presented itself, as we were invited to perform the trial at Manchaca United Methodist Church. Manchaca is just outside the hip, cosmopolitan city of Austin, but it felt like a different world. The church where we would do the trial, Manchaca United Methodist, is on a street called "Farm to Market 1626." The church members were remarkably generous. Some used their frequent-flier miles to get us to Texas, and others volunteered to put us up in their homes. Joy's hosts were most memorable; the husband was a prosecutor, and the woman carried a small pink pistol in her purse.

The night before, we met at a Mexican restaurant with Abby Rapoport and her husband, Sam, who lived in Austin. Like many of the best places to eat in Texas, it was an informal joint, and we sat at a picnic table under an awning out back. The smell of carnitas was intoxicating. The waitress came to get our orders, and when it was Jeanne's turn, she asked, "What kind of white wine do you have?" The waitress rolled her eyes, and Joy said, "What the hell, Jeanne!" Jeanne had lived in Texas for two years as a child, but in the wealthy enclave of Highland Park near Dallas. Later, she did spend her high school years in Oklahoma City, and as a homecoming princess at Northwestern University she appeared in the parade waving a cowboy hat, but none of this directed her away from Joy's drawled approbation.

On the way to the church, we drove by a field of cattle, which Jeanne and Joy couldn't resist jumping out to see. Jeanne jumped out because she was clueless, and Joy, because she was reckless. I declined to join them, as I knew that ranchers could be very protective of their livestock, and the livestock could be violent themselves. I stayed in the car as they strolled through a pasture dotted with cow dung. "What a weird life I have," I thought as I saw them get too close to a longhorn. I was about to jump out of the car and warn them off when I saw a Ford F-250 dually (a pickup truck with dual wheels on the rear axle) head slowly down the dirt road from the ranch house to the field. Panicked, I tried to call Joy on her cell phone, but she did not pick up—service is patchy in rural Texas.

It was like watching a train wreck in slow motion. I imagined the ranchers, armed to the teeth, confronting the two women in their field. In horror, I saw the truck pull up to where they were, and Joy trotted over to the driver's side. Then the truck slowly trundled back to where it came from. When Joy and Jeanne got back to the car to my look of bemusement, Joy shrugged and said, "I handled it."

The fields around the church were spread with something else: swaths of bluebonnets, the state flower of Texas, mixed with another wildflower, Indian paintbrush, or prairie-fire. By the side of the road, we could see small groups of people—parents with children, young lovers—crouched in the midst of the sea of blue, red, and gold, taking pictures. I imagined Stephen running through the color like a blur and looked straight ahead as I bit my lower lip.

"What are they doing?" Jeanne asked, looking out the open window of the car as I sped up. Joy and I knew: taking your portrait in the center of a field of bluebonnets was a Texas tradition. At Jeanne's insistence, we got out of the car to crouch down in the field of glorious color while Jeanne snapped our photo. I smiled, despite the painful vision of Stephen. It was wonderful to be outside on a gorgeous spring day in a field of bluebonnets; I suppose that at least part of my heart had been left in Texas, and I was there to reclaim it. In the picture, Joy is leaning on me, both of her arms encircling me as we look at the camera.

We also were going to use some local talent. James Nortey, the Harvard Law grad who now was working in Austin for a law firm, agreed to be our judge—the first black judge in our project's history. Our other addition was Kent McKeever, the man we had met up with at the coffee shop in Nashville. He had, as promised, moved to Waco and founded a legal services office. He also served as a youth minister at my old church, Seventh and James Baptist. For Lent, Kent had embarked on a remarkable project that was completely consistent with my own spiritual pull. He explained it to me in an e-mail as he pondered his actions:

> I have been thinking about wearing an orange jumpsuit (prisoner attire) every day during Lent. My heart continues to break over and over again at the devastation caused by our War on Drugs and mass incarceration system and "tough on crime" attitude and policy. . . . The countless other ways our world locks up the poor and marginalized . . . compels me to do something visible to bring attention to the issues and especially to the plight of chains of our own making. Talking about it isn't enough.

My first response to his idea was less than encouraging—I told him that he might get shot by someone who mistook him for an escapee from the jail. He was not dissuaded, though. For those forty days, he wore an orange prison jumpsuit everywhere that he went and wrote about it on a blog titled *40 Days in Orange*.

Within a week of the trial in Manchaca, I moderated a panel on clemency at NYU. By chance, I sat down at a table for lunch at the symposium with both White House Counsel Kathy Ruemmler and Jesse Wegman, a member of the editorial board at the *New York Times*. I suppose I should have been pressing Ruemmler for action on clemency, but I instantly found myself deep in conversation with Wegman, who was wonderfully conversant on the things I cared about. When I mentioned Kent, his eyes lit up, and on April 18 there was a remarkable piece about the man in a prison uniform on the Opinion page of the *Times*. At its heart, Jesse Wegman's piece captured in a few lines the theology Kent was living:

> For Mr. McKeever, the days of Lent and Easter—the emergence of life from death, as he puts it—are the perfect time to highlight these issues. "There are certainly consequences of our sins," he said. "But what do we want for that person who has broken the law? Do we want to just respond with punishment and condemnation, or do we want to try to redeem and rehabilitate and help bring goodness and life and love out of that?"[1]

There was something thrilling about seeing this transgressive faith laid out so plainly in the *New York Times*, complete with a photo of Kent pushing a cart in the supermarket, attired in his prison uniform.

Though Kent was a lawyer with a degree from Vanderbilt, I chose not to make him my second chair. Instead, he would be Jesus—becoming the precise physical embodiment of Christ's teaching that when we visit the prisoner, we see Jesus himself.

We were to present the trial the afternoon of Palm Sunday. It was, again, a day fraught with meaning: the anniversary of the murder of Jeanne's sister. To get to know the church better, I decided to go to both of the services at Manchaca United Methodist Church that morning. The first was a praise music service, and the second was more traditional. I snuck in a little late to the first service, which was full of younger people and families. A band was pounding out tunes at the front of the social hall where the service was held, and with a start I noticed something shocking: Joy Tull was playing the drums for the worship band.

I suppose that it shouldn't have surprised me; I knew that Joy is a talented percussionist. However, it wasn't the "band" part that

---

1. Jesse Wegman, "An Orange Jumpsuit for Lent," *New York Times*, April 18, 2014.

surprised me; it was the "worship" part. I knew that her presence didn't represent a healing of Joy's relationship with God in one fell swoop, but it did show me that there was a small part of church where she felt comfortable. When I got over my surprise, I started to clap along.

The second service was nearly as remarkable. It simply recounted the story of Holy Week, as one after another of the parishioners rose to read the story of those seven days from the Gospels. Old and young, they took their turns in voices shaky and strong; there was something deeply affecting about it. The readers were scattered among the audience and did not go to the altar to read. Instead, they stood where they were and read from there as the audience swiveled in their seats to spot their voices. I loved the idea of the sermon coming entirely from the congregation in the pews. The familiar story, told in this new way, settled my heart as I prepared to prosecute Jesus.

As we rearranged the furniture in the early afternoon, James Nortey arrived on cue. He had brought his mother and a robe with green and gold stripes on one sleeve; it was his uniform from his days as the chief justice at the student court at Baylor. Soon Joy was chatting with James's mom as I went over the procedures for the trial with him. After the aberrational rules in Arizona, it was good to return to the more-familiar Texas procedure, where the key question for the jury rested on the perceived future dangerousness of the defendant.

Meanwhile, Jeanne began to go over testimony with the man slated to play the crucial role of Peter. As we expected to find with our Texas witnesses, he was remarkably biblically literate and understood the broad sweep of the story we were telling. He confided to Jeanne that he was, in fact, an opponent of the death penalty and often felt isolated in that community, where sentiment in favor of capital punishment ran high. The minister, in a brief conversation between services, told us that she "was a little worried" about how it would be received in her politically conservative congregation, but I wasn't worried. These were the people we needed to speak to, and it wasn't our first rodeo.

The trial began with James Nortey swearing in the jurors. Sitting at counsel table next to Joy, I watched their faces as they raised their hands and recited the oath. They seemed earnest, as if they were taking the project seriously. I resolved to do the same. After Joy completed her opening, I called Peter to the stand, my red Bible in my hand for reference.

I knew he could follow each verse I referred to, so I set my notes aside and led him through my points. There was a moment in the middle of the methodical process when I stopped. It may have been only for a split second, but in my memory it was an eternity as I stood there silently. I was stopped by a thought: that the defendant behind me was the only one who would have known what lies beyond death. I wanted to turn to him and ask; to find out where it was that Jeanne's relatives and Katherine Darmer and Stephen were now. I wanted them to be loved.

It was only a moment, though. I reverted to role and continued as a prosecutor. Something, however, had happened. Just as fourteen years before I had found that I didn't want to be a federal prosecutor anymore, I knew that I didn't want to do this anymore, either. There was too much death. I wanted to get back to the Jesus who walked with his friends and then sat and taught.

But first I had to finish this. I changed my closing this time and ended not with a warning about impending death and the danger of Jesus but with something else that reflected the weariness of my soul. I told them, instead, that my work, criminal law, is all about tragedy. Even if I do my job as a prosecutor in the best way possible, perfectly even, that does not mean that a murder victim is unkilled or a woman unraped. Too often, we just create new tragedies on top of the ones that have already happened. The best that we can hope for is to avoid tragedies in the future through the actions we take today. And then I stopped. It was enough.

In the now-familiar pattern, the church members gathered into groups of twelve and began to talk. I felt calm but spent. Jesus/Kent was talking to Jeanne, and Joy was dashing around distributing verdict forms. Meanwhile, I snuck out the side entrance. There was a driveway and beyond that a field of bluebonnets, like the stars in the sky in Minnesota. I sat on the edge of the field listening to the wind and the pickup trucks passing now and then on Farm-to-Market Road 1626 until it was time to go back for the verdicts. I had been in this same position, waiting, in so many places: in the warm air of Richmond and the chill of Massachusetts, in tears at Carson-Newman, under the palms in California, in the damp swamp of anger in Louisiana, and in the dry, hot dusk in Arizona. Perhaps I had to find a new way to listen to Jesus, who had been there all along.

So I went back inside. As was so often true, the discussion of the juries was the most important part of the exercise. That reflected a truth I recognized as a young lawyer: that for all our skills, we will not be there for the most important discussion of all in a jury trial. This was no different. As the forepersons spoke, they uniformly talked about conflicting beliefs and emotions in themselves and their group. When they were done, we answered questions. For the first time, many of the questions were for Jesus, as the parishioners wanted to know more about his project. Kent answered each question with kindness.

Then we were done. Jeanne, Joy, Kent, and I stood on the gravel outside as the crowd dispersed. Joy looked around. "You guys hungry?" she asked. "Let's go to Sonic." She pointed to a Sonic Drive-In just down the road, one of the few businesses in the tiny town. So we did.

The Sonic was on a cement pad by the side of the road, surrounded by a gas station on one side and pastureland on the other. At parking spots lining the building there were speakerphones and menu boards, and a few tables were set out in the middle. We sat down at a round plastic table and ordered some limeade and tater tots. We must have looked like an odd group; I was still in my suit while Kent was wearing his orange prison jumpsuit with matching bright-orange prison shoes. In the cars parked nearby, a few people looked over warily. It was that way for Jesus, too; people were drawn to him, and the Gospels are populated with strangers who approach him or watch from afar.

In that moment, for the first time in nearly a year, I felt at peace. I knew what my next step would be, in work and in spirit. Weary from the trial, we took turns telling stories and laughing; Joy ate most of the tater tots. On the road, there was only an occasional car or truck, and I saw at least one slow down to look at Kent.

"Do you worry?" I asked him, remembering my initial advice to him that warned of the danger of getting shot.

He shrugged. "Everything is a risk," he said. I knew he was right. After all, I was at a conservative church in rural Texas to prosecute

Jesus. Then he started to talk about one of our clients, Homar Fajardo. He was from Waco, and Kent had met his wife, Marie, who had prayed for her husband and driven hundreds of miles to see him. Kent talked about them as people, as whole, as loved.

Just then, two teenage boys were making their way to the front of the building. As they started to go around our table, they froze. They had seen Kent, and his appearance had stopped them cold—they were at that age where your body follows your mind with every instinctual reaction. An adult might have kept going, looking out of the corner of an eye and whispering later to a friend, but at fifteen you just stop and stare.

Kent looked up. He has gentle features and a full beard even in the heat of a Texas spring. He met their eyes. The two boys said nothing. Nor did they move. Joy looked as though she was about to interject, but I stopped her with a glance. I had seen Jesus.

Jeanne and Joy looked on anxiously. Leaning forward in his prison uniform, Kent smiled and nodded at the two boys, who were still frozen in place. "So," he asked, "do you want to hear the story?"

CPSIA information can be obtained
at www.ICGtesting.com
Printed in the USA
LVOW04s0201160816

500510LV00015B/130/P